Pelican Books
The NHS: Your Money or Your Life

Lesley Garner is a freelance journalist whose
articles, including those on the National Health
Service, have appeared in such newspapers as the
Sunday Times. With her husband, a specialist in
paediatrics and tropical public health, she has
travelled widely in many underdeveloped countries,
and has used this experience in her analysis of the
varying problems of medical care delivery.

'This momentous book will rank as the contemporary successor to the classic works of Booth and Rowntree; its case histories alone should put paid to those who still assert that there is no longer poverty in Britain' – Barbara Wooton

Poverty in the United Kingdom
A survey of household resources and standards of living
Peter Townsend

'The chief conclusion of this report is that poverty is more extensive than is generally or officially believed, and has to be understood not only as an inevitable feature of severe social inequality but also as a particular consequence of actions by the rich to preserve and enhance their wealth and so deny it to others . . . The extremely unequal distribution of wealth is perhaps the single most notable feature of social conditions in the United Kingdom.'

Professor Townsend's massive and controversial survey is the most comprehensive investigation into poverty and wealth in Britain ever undertaken. It has virtually the scope and prestige of a Royal Commission, and will stand as the seminal work on the subject for years to come.

'Not only presents the results of the most extensive survey of poverty carried out in Britain, but also brings together Townsend's thinking over the last 25 years on the subject of poverty, the position of social minorities, and the role of social institutions. It is a veritable tour de force.' – *Guardian*

'The contribution to knowledge and understanding is great indeed, and covers so many topics and correlations that it will provide material for discussion for years to come.' – *New Society*

Lesley Garner

The NHS: Your Money or Your Life

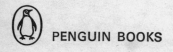

PENGUIN BOOKS

Penguin Books Ltd, Harmondsworth,
Middlesex, England
Penguin Books, 625 Madison Avenue,
New York, New York 10022, U.S.A.
Penguin Books Australia Ltd, Ringwood,
Victoria, Australia
Penguin Books Canada Ltd, 2801 John Street,
Markham, Ontario, Canada L3R 1B4
Penguin Books (N.Z.) Ltd, 182–190 Wairau Road,
Auckland 10, New Zealand

First published 1979
Copyright © Lesley Garner, 1979
All rights reserved

Set, printed and bound in Great Britain by
Cox & Wyman Ltd, Reading
Set in Intertype Times

Contents

Acknowledgements

Many people have helped me with this book, including many NHS employees directly quoted in it, and some of these prefer to remain anonymous. But particular thanks for pointing me in their direction are due to Mr Gillies at the DHSS, Gordon Beverly of North-East Thames Region, Victor Ripley of North-West Thames, John Every of the Oxford Region, Pat Torrie of the King's Fund College, Dr Mike d'Souza of St Thomas's Hospital Department of Community Medicine, Derek Hull of Trent Region and the librarians of the British Medical Association, the King's Fund College and the King's Fund Centre, and the Health Education Council. Most of the many facts and figures about the NHS come from DHSS statistics and are to be found in HMSO publications. I have given no references for these. The most thanks are due to my husband, Dr Ken Grant, for practical help, for reading the manuscript and for arguing with me.

1 The Health Service Disease

The National Health Service is bankrupt. The National Health Service is on the brink of collapse. The National Health Service is no more than a vast and ruined city of dilapidated buildings, whose echoing corridors are walked by the exhausted wraiths of underpaid doctors and nurses, stalked by blood-sucking vampires in the mild, deceitful guise of grey health service administrators, and haunted by the wistful spectres of departed patients who, after years in queues and waiting lists have passively given up the ghost. Whatever clouds of glory the NHS may have trailed at its birth in 1948 have dispersed. If we are to believe the chorus of despair which harmonizes its song of doom from every quarter, the health service, the pride and joy of the Welfare State, has proved itself to be an impossible dream.

It would be foolish to deny that a state of crisis exists, but what the emotional power of the chorus disguises is the fact that the crisis is not new to the NHS. Despite the idealism that saw its birth in the post-war years, Aneurin Bevan, for one, knew that he was launching a dream with an innate capacity to become a nightmare. He felt it was worth launching anyway. 'It [postponement] is stupid nonsense,' he told a meeting of nurses in 1948. 'We never will have all we need. Expectation will always exceed capacity.'[1] And his realism was borne out by Enoch Powell, a Minister of Health at a different time and of a different party, who remarked dryly that one of the most striking features of the NHS was the deafening chorus of complaint which rose from it day and night:

a chorus only interrupted when someone suggests that a different system altogether might be preferable, which would involve the money coming from some less (literally) palpable source. The universal exchequer financing of the service endows everyone providing it as well as everyone using it with a vested interest in denigrating it, so that it presents what must be the unique spectacle of an undertaking that is run down by everyone engaged in it.[2]

Thirty years after its birth the situation is no more satisfactory and the voices have not been stilled. What is ignored by most of the critics, both inside the service and out of it, is that the current failings of our health service are not something peculiarly and privately the property of Britain or of the Welfare State. In the light of its own ideals, the NHS is simply the most visible example of an epidemic of crisis which is threatening every health service in the world, regardless of economic or political bias. The classic symptoms of the health service disease are an acute shortage of money and resources to meet the growing demands placed upon the service, low morale and a notable lack of unified purpose among health service workers, catastrophic shortfall of provision in both cure and care so that the services – state and private – fall across the population like a moth-eaten blanket, killing some of its citizens with kindness and leaving the majority to suffer from exposure. On the one hand health services have to cope with a shortage of adequate buildings and hardware; on the other they can find their budgets gnawed to the bone by the voracious demands of spanking new hospitals and runaway technology. Increasingly they find themselves unable to cope either with the pressures created by a growing theoretical ability to work scientific miracles, or with the problems created by the overwhelming demand of vast numbers of people for simple, basic improvements in the day-to-day quality of their lives.

A combination of some or all of these symptoms is currently to be found in every health service in the world, from the United States of America where money can buy the best available health care, to the most impoverished Third World country where 90% of the population may never meet a health worker at any level from birth to death – a distance which may be very short indeed. In every country, whatever the course the health service disease takes, the root causes are the same – an increasingly impossible struggle between supply and demand.

This insoluble conflict has been intensified by increased political awareness, by the refusal of people in developed countries to be offered less than the best they know exists. The last fifty years have seen a universal acceptance of health care as a basic human right, rather than as a privilege or a purchasable luxury, and this concept has put strong pressure on governments to make adequate provision of health services to the population. Add to this the rocketing potential of medicine to perform spectacular but phenomenally expensive sleights of hand, and you end up with an impossible balancing act between expectation and resources. What nobody, whether politician, professional or public, will willingly admit is that there is no way to balance the equation. It is self-perpetuating, and if it were to be otherwise, then it would demand an ability to pour forth money in quantities beyond the current capacity of government or individual.

Rather than face the public with an explicit choice, governments desperately try to make ends meet. Developed countries in particular have been drawn into spending increasing amounts of money on their health services. In 1957, the United States spent 3.5% of its gross national product on health, in 1968 it was 6·6% and by 1980 it will have reached between 8% and 10%. It is far from being the only Western country that is on its way to spending 10% of all it has on its health. In France expenditure on medical care has grown twice as fast as the GNP (Gross National Product) over the last ten years, and estimates suggest that by 1985 it will be spending up to 13% of a doubled GNP. In Britain our current 6% is expected to rise to 8·5% by 1980. In 1949 it was 4%.

The fact is that the NHS, far from starving away, has grown fatter – or at least better fed – year by year. In 1976 the annual budget for the health and personal social services was £6,200 million, an increase of 15% on the previous year, which, in its turn, was 32% higher than the year before that. Even allowing for inflation, expenditure on health and social services in England and Wales has more than doubled in the last twenty years. Since its inception the health service has increased its overall staff by 75%, although the population at large has increased by only 6%, and it now employs nearly one million people – a growth rate and a size that makes its employees joke wearily that if it continues to grow at its present rate, by the year 2000 every working member of the community would be employed by it in some capacity or other.

The assumption on which the NHS was founded was the very opposite to this relentless growth. The idea was that the country lay beneath a stagnant pool of untreated sickness and that once the new health service had applied itself diligently, the remainder of its task would be a kind of inexpensive maintenance of standards. Everything that has happened since has put this theory on a level with Canute's law of tide control. The health service is better fed but it is infested with tapeworms. Demand is a hydra. Lop off one gaping head and two more sprout in its place, nourished by continually changing concepts of what health services can and should do. No sooner are the hazards of childhood and early infancy overcome than we are faced with the demands of handicap and lingering, expensive old age. Each time an effective treatment is uncovered for a hitherto neglected and hopeless problem, such as renal failure, then the sufferers from that ailment cease to be doomed and become a pool of aggressively demanding customers. Where there is hope, there is life. And as each serious medical problem becomes placated with treatment, the remaining problems become more and more expensive and complex to solve. As the diseases associated with poverty, poor housing and malnutrition become part of history, diseases associated with affluence, materialism and high living spring up in their place. We no longer die of tuberculosis in Victorian slums, but we can eat and smoke ourselves to death instead.

The most insoluble part of the problems springs from the way we think. The existence of a National Health Service carries a political promise that we will no longer be expected to put up with things, but the things up with which we will not put become more and more intractable. In the absence of social, religious and moral guardians, the health services have become the focus of demand for all kinds of social and psychological needs. These are fairly clear-cut in the case of the old, of the mentally and physically handicapped, but infinitely vague and complex in the case of the rest of us who present the doctor with a broken marriage in the guise of a backache, a frustrating job disguised as asthma, or a fear of the future clothed in sleeplessness. This presentation of every kind of problem to the health service is encouraged by the press who tend to devote such space as they give to medicine to scandals of neglect on the one hand, and the vaunting of miracles on the other. Hardly a piece of advice on any kind of human problem is printed in newspaper or magazine, but that it ends with the words 'see your family doctor'.

In the absence of other doorsteps – including our own individual ones – on which to lay our doubts, fears, neuroses and minor ailments, the health service is expected to provide a doorstep manned by sympathetic watchmen day and night. If it is not so manned we become upset. Those of us who become most upset, who knock most often at the door with the greatest confidence of being answered, are the articulate, the middle-class, the educated, the young. It is this group who get most out of the health service, not necessarily those with the greatest need, but those who are best equipped to make their demands clear. As populations in general become better educated and more demanding, this group of articulate consumers will grow.

One of the dilemmas off which this demand feeds is the fact that nobody has actually laid down what a health service is *for*. The National Health Service Act of 1946 proclaimed the duty of the Minister of Health to be the promotion of 'a comprehensive health service designed to secure improvement in the physical and mental health of the people of England and Wales and the prevention, diagnosis and treatment of illness . . .' But what is health? The assumption behind the promise is that sickness is an absolute state not, as it is turning out to be in practice 'a relative state capable of infinite interpretation'. In making this rod to beat their own backs the writers of the National Health Service Act were joined by the distinguished World

Health Organizations whose utopian definition of health makes invalids of us all. 'Health,' according to the body whose scope ranges from the lepers of Leopoldville to the neurotics of New York City, 'is a state of complete physical, mental and social well-being and not merely the absence of disease and infirmity.' Since, by this definition, 99% of the world's population must be in need of care and attention, the World Health Organization has simply written itself into existence for eternity.

The concept of what an ill person is changes from minute to minute, and even once such a person has been identified and agreed to be in need of care by those responsible for supplying it, the options for treatment are enormously varied and include the option of no treatment at all. If care is needed, is it needed at any price? Is it needed if supplying it means denying someone else whose need might be greater? Is it needed if the person concerned is largely responsible for his own condition? Is it needed if the person is, in any case, on the point of death through old age? Is it needed if arresting this particular condition means that the individual survives as a crippled dependant? Is it needed, not because it will materially improve the patient's condition, but because something will have been seen to have been done? For all its proven and spectacular successes much medicine is shot with the colour of primitive and placatory ritual.

However, if all these definitions of health and ill health and need lead to unrealistic expectations from us, the professionals who man health services are no less idealistic. The demand which comes from the consumer is no more voracious than the demands set up within a health service. The enormously high, and perhaps unrealistic, standards set by the best of Western medicine are a growing problem to us, and even more of a problem to poorer countries where they have been transplanted to an alien soil with troubling results. Scientific research extends the horizons of what can be done almost daily. As soon as the horizon has moved a large number of people feel they must instantly reach it and the medical profession is largely on their side.

It cannot be stated too clearly that a doctor who faces, one to one, a patient for whom a treatment is available, however expensive, is under every kind of emotional, professional and social pressure to use that treatment whatever the political or economic argument may be against it. This is particularly so in a system like the NHS where the state has guaranteed, regardless of cost, to provide the best treatment available for each citizen according to need. If the doctor faces the patient a thousand miles from the source of the treatment, then the pressure on him is relieved. If he works in a system where the treatment will be available only if the patient himself can pay for it, then the pressure is likewise reduced. But where the doctor feels the pressure, it will be intensified by the natural irritation he feels towards any politician or administrator – far from the patient's bedside and from any personal turmoil of pain or anxiety – who tells him he must not or cannot provide the treatment. From this conflict between the front line and the staff springs all kinds of hostility, resentment, dissatisfaction and discontent. It is this conflict between the personal and the universal that is at the root of a nation's disposal of health care.

The Western doctor has been educated to believe that his decision on medical matters is sacrosanct, that his clinical freedom is absolute and that, where possible, nothing but the best should be provided for his patients. He has not been taught to consider cost, and he relies on other deterrents such as queues and long waiting times to do some of his rationing, impersonally, for him. What medicine can theoretically do expands every day. However, the responsibility for providing resources rests, not with the individual doctor, but with the state, which, having publicly taken the responsibility for supplying unlimited quantities of health care, has made itself into a visible scapegoat. Nobody likes to say that the supply is limited, but someone, somewhere along the line, has to make the decisions which will turn the money this way or that.

The cost of modern medicine is astronomical. Other countries may invest more heavily than Britain in medical hardware, in EMI scanners at £300,000 each, in special units for open heart surgery or renal dialysis, but everywhere the suppliers of medical care are up against the realization that some kind of end is at hand. Health may be a good thing, but it cannot expand indefinitely in competition with all the other good things that modern societies expect to enjoy: with education, with defence, with the social services, with law and order, with the arts, agriculture and housing. What sets health apart from all these other competing needs is its enormous emotional power. There is a direct link between shortages in health care and acute human suffering. If the ambulance service is on strike, if the accident and emergency department has been closed or there are no staff to run the children's ward, then victims will immediately be found. And on top of this pile will be the consultant arguing that if he had this or that piece of equipment, lives would be saved. Someone who wants to build a new road could use the same argument, but he will find it harder to pinpoint his potential victim. The medical profession has no shortage of them.

The most immediately visible effect of these shortages and stresses in the health service is the low morale produced in health workers. This can mean short tempers in an overworked hospital ward where staff are stretched from a heavy workload and lack of sleep. It can mean bitter disagreements between different groups of workers such as health service unions and doctors, or doctors and administrators. It can mean constant grousing at every level about bureaucrats and politicians. For a patient it can mean the gradual transformation, in time, of a relatively simple condition into an emergency.

'It's brought home to us,' explained the administrator of a district general hospital in a country town, 'because of the intense pressure on everybody. Everything comes here and we've got to process it under the pressure of so many emergencies. Everyone is at each other's throats. The pressure is too great in pathology, for example, so they've simply reduced the service. They've asked the clinicians for help and said, "Please look at the way you ask for tests." ' To this a colleague added:

It sounds silly, but to get into this hospital you're really got to be ill. This place is turning more and more into a giant intensive care unit. We can't stop emergencies. It's a question of the population in certain areas having a certain number of beds. The population here has gone up and we have a lot of old people and the hospital just isn't coping. The nurses are so hard-stretched that there's an endless non-stop crisis. The average stay in the ward here is three days – we move them on after that. 85% occupancy at night means 100% occupancy during the day – sometimes 125% – that's a hell of a pressure and the staffing establishment is funded to 85% occupancy. Staff are supposed to survive by having peaks and troughs, but here there aren't any.

The immediate gut reaction to this – the reaction of press, unions, politicians and public – is to demand more money instantly. The response is emotionally based and entirely understandable. If the health service is running at such a danger level because it is short of money, then money is what it needs. But as we have already seen, such money as has been allocated to it – a 20% increase over five years, £5 thousand million a year, £250 a year for every household – vanishes like frost in the sun. The alternative, or at least the prerequisite, is to look very closely at the way the money is spent. Maybe half the tests it carried out were unnecessary. Because of the ethical problems involved, the regular and ruthless evaluation of medical treatments and procedures has traditionally been treated with suspicion throughout most of the medical profession, but economic and social conditions are changing that. Slowly, under pressure, the idea that all health practices are equally valuable is being questioned, and the concept of cost-effectiveness is being gradually introduced.

One of the basic reasons why more money is not the only answer to the problem is that good health does not come solely from more health care. In fact many people question the relevance of health services to health. The great improvements in health over the last century come, not from better hospitals or more sophisticated surgical techniques, but from better working conditions, improved sanitation and nutrition, proper housing and clean water supplies. The United States spends more money on health care than any other country in the world, but its mortality figures fail to reflect the high level of investment. In fact the results of a multi-national survey showed that the United States came out worst. Perinatal deaths per 1,000 were 1·7 in Sweden, 8·0 in England and Wales, 13·0 in Scotland and 15·3 in the United States.[3] The same figures show the discrepancy within the British Isles, between mortality levels in Scotland, England and Wales. Scotland spends proportionately more on its health service than England and Wales, but its mortality figures – the traditional and, so far, the only universally accepted measure of success – show no benefit from the extra cash. The blame for this is traditionally put on the lower quality of housing in Scotland. Maybe the logical step for the Scottish Home and Health Department to take is to switch its resources from hospitals to houses.

The organization that faces this complexity of problems is itself very complex. In Britain, where the health service is an apparently monolithic government body with a unique responsibility, it might be assumed to be unified and of one purpose, but within the million-strong population of the NHS are dozens of separate and competing interests. Far from being united by a single focus, which the rest of us naïvely suppose to be the patient, the different professions within the health service are driven as much by self-interest as by any common concept or purpose. The pressures on consultant heart surgeons are not at all the same as those on student nurses, on radiographers or on the members of NUPE (National Union of Public Employees). Despite being there, theoretically, to carry out the ideals and aims laid down by a Labour government after the Second World War, the employees of the health service share neither politics, ideal concepts of health care, economic background, social background, hope for the future or even mutual respect. But because they all share one employer, blame for whatever goes wrong can easily be laid at the enormous door leading to the labyrinth that is the National Health Service. More accurately, since it is very difficult to blame any one individual within the service, blame is laid at the door of whichever politician happens to be Minister of Health at the time, an individual who, as health service employees say bitterly, might well be the Minister of Agriculture and Fisheries the following week.

Responsibility and blame for the failing of the health service are otherwise distributed confusingly among the other employees, with certain traditional scapegoats. Doctors, it is worth noting, are rarely blamed. Nurses never. Administrators are criticized constantly and forcefully, the more so for their being faceless and consequently ominous, and because, although there are so many of them, their function is not immediately apparent to the average reporter or member of the public, or even to the other workers in the health service. The increasingly vocal health service unions are also criticized because they are all too often seen to put their members' interests above the interests of the patients. The last person to receive any brickbats, interestingly enough, is the individual patient who, in a society where the worst health problems are increasingly due to individual behaviour, may very well be held to blame for being ill in the first place and consequently for wasting all our money.

A great many of the problems of the health service come from the conflict of interest and power between the many groups involved in dispensing health care, and in particular from the fading of traditional voices and the rising power of quite new ones. In the absence of clear lines of responsibility from any other source, the strongest voice in the disposition of health services has traditionally been the medical voice. The medical point of view, despite what doctors may claim to the contrary, is not necessarily identical with the interests of the patient. In many ways it cuts across them. The intoxication of medical glamour clings to procedures which may prove to be, if not harmful, at best useless. No less a person than Dr Mahler, Director of the World Health Organization, is on record as saying that 'the major and most expensive part of medical technology as applied today appears to be more for the satisfaction of the health professionals than for the benefit of the consumers . . .'⁴ In other countries the bias of modern medicine has effects even more obviously distorting to the health services as a whole, than they are in a tightly budgeted system like the NHS. In the poor countries of the Third World, for example, the hospitals and equipment which doctors have been taught to think necessary to the practice of good medicine can eat up ludicrously disproportionate quantities of a national health budget, leaving literally nothing for the vast majority of people who live outside the range and scope of these centres of excellence.

The problem in these countries and in the developed world is the same in essence if not degree. Clinical freedom, which is at the root of every doctor's commitment to his profession and his individual responsibility to his patient, leads to far-reaching decisions, both medical and economic, being taken in complete isolation from the health needs of the population as a whole. It is useless for planners to plan and managers to manage, for priorities to be laid down at ministry level, and for political decisions to be taken on the disposition of health care to the people, when the individual decision of the individual doctor is sacrosanct. The great dilemma is that whereas health services are responsible for the health of whole populations, doctors are not and never have been. Their responsibility is to meet the demands of their individual patients as far as they can. And whether they supply kind words, a placebo, a course of drugs, or a hospital referral leading to extremely expensive surgery, is up to them. Any threat to clinical freedom leads doctors to mutter darkly about being state employees and medical puppets, but clinical freedom is just as likely to lead to bad decisions as to good ones. It is quite possible for a hospital which is besieged with cases to be carrying out unnecessary or inappropriate treatment as well as vital care. And in a world where the choice of treatment becomes more complex and the guidelines less clear – particularly in the field of prescribing – there is a growing case for some kind of centralized system of evaluation and advice.

Because doctors are trained as healers they affect the bias of modern health services towards acute, curative medicine and away from prevention or long-term care. In countries where there is less centralized control than there is in the British health service, this leads to a total absence of services for certain geographic areas and for whole classes of patients. Even in the NHS, despite continued directives, papers and memos from the Department of Health, it leads to neglect of certain geographic areas and to a visibly second-class service for whole groups of patients such as the mentally ill and handicapped, the old and the chronically sick. Clinical freedom concentrates doctors in the areas they find most rewarding, both professionally and economically, but it restricts the service to the population as a whole.

Because of these deeply conflicting interests among health service employees, because of the enormously increasing public demand upon it and the multiplicity of pressures from within and without, those responsible for the NHS – and for health services throughout the world – are becoming increasingly aware of the need for what is disparagingly called state interference – or what might, more politely, be called long-term planning. Services which grow up unplanned do not grow freely into a pattern of admirable equity and universally high quality. Like plants seeking the light, they tend to crowd all their efforts into certain tight corners and leave others completely exposed. The people who despair most publicly of the failings of the NHS have often been heard to say, as a clincher, that if it is so wonderful, why hasn't every country in the world followed our example? One answer to that is that to a certain extent, they have. It is now universally recognized, éven in countries as firmly committed to the concept of free enterprise and self-sufficiency as the United States, that a free-for-all in health care, with its astonishing potential for infinite specialization, cost and exploitation, results in appalling inadequacies and inequalities of service for all but the very privileged. It leads to duplication of very expensive facilities and their consequent under- and misuse. It leads to competition which benefits nobody, and to great gulfs and chasms of neglect between sunlit plateaus of perfect, if expensive, care. If a government is to accept any kind of responsibility for the health of a nation, then an element of central control is vital. It says a great deal about the strength of the competing influences that, given thirty years of state health services in Britain, so many of these inequities and injustices are still so evident in the NHS. For thirty years it has struggled forward from the base provided for it by nine-teenth century hospitals, asylums and almshouses and has expanded, like a coral, from these uneven Victorian roots. The days of this expansion, such as it is, are over.

There is a growing and explicit recognition that health care, once a sacred trust in the hands of the medically qualified few – who delivered it to the few – has been encroached upon by other sectors in society. This means not only must health compete openly with other social needs such as housing and education, but there must be a much more open refereeing of the competition which has always existed, if covertly, within the health service itself. It should be declared openly and unequivocally that the provision of a coronary care unit in one district now means the closure of a maternity ward in another, that one million pounds allotted to an old peoples' day care centre means one million pounds less on research into the causes of cancer. Traditionally the most prestigious consultants have continued to build their empires by winning resources from the less pre-stigious. Individual voices and medical tradition have always counted for a great deal in the way our health budget has been spent. With the advent of overt priorities and planning, and the growth of administration, the theory is that the hundreds of separate competing interests are being set against each other according to a predetermined set of values, not simply accord-ing to the panic of the moment or the latest technological ad-vance. This upheaval is deeply upsetting to the sectors of the health service at whose expense it is being carried out, and to the public which sees only a diminution of the service without being aware of the forces and choices behind it. It is no longer enough to punch home the emotional argument. Decisions must be openly made that were covertly made before, and they will be very difficult decisions. The dilemma was put very succinctly by a health service administrator who is faced daily by impossible claims on his budget:

You ask people 'What kind of health service do you want?' and they say 'the best'. But the community must realize that there is a cost to everything. That basically there is a price on human life. They must realize that there is a limit. They must look at what value they place on the health service as opposed to any of the other public services like education or social services. Personally, I would like to see outside every hospital a big board saying 'This hospital costs so many thousand pounds a day,' and in every ward the same. Then it would be easier to enter into an argument on priorities. High technology medicine is very expensive and people should realize the cost. Even the most minimal development that people suggest to me can cost £1,000. So I ask them where we can get it from. Do we put up income tax? Do we lose some other service? I'm always met with absolute silence. People forget there is a price.

2 A Purchasable Commodity

Health ... is a purchasable commodity of which a community can possess, within limits, as much or as little as it cares to pay for. It can turn its resources in one direction and fifty thousand of its members will live who would otherwise have died; it can turn them in another and fifty thousand will die who would otherwise have lived. Though no individual, by taking thought, can add a cubit to his stature, a nation, by doing so, can add an inch to the height of some groups among its children and a pound to their weight.[1]

So wrote the historian R. H. Tawney in 1931, before the establishment of the NHS, but health is no less of a commodity today than it was fifty years ago. Every unit of health care carries an invisible price tag. In a free market system the problem is out in the open. If you can pay the price you can have the treatment. If you can't, you can do without. In a system like the National Health Service where the government has accepted the responsibility of providing, and the load is spread throughout the community by means of taxation, the price tag is still there but the decision to pay it is not made by the individual. A covert and complicated system of rationing operates, none the less effective because most of us prefer not to think that it exists. The very notion of a National Health Service implies the promise that rationing is abolished. Health care, instead of being a service we can buy or not, as we need it, has become an inalienable human right, lifted somehow above the competition and squalor of the market-place. In fact health care even behaves economically like more obvious consumer durables such as washing-machines and television sets. The richer the country the more it spends on health. Instead of good health increasing with the rise in national income, it is spending on health that rises. In Britain this harsh commercial reality has been hidden. Instead of operating in an open market, the processes of choice and rationing have been driven underground.

One reason for this is the enormous difficulty of deciding the choices that have to be made. At its crudest, the disposition of a million pounds here or there can mean life or death to the groups of patients who are catered for or are neglected. Extra investment into cancer research means further delay in research into tissue-typing for bone marrow disease. An accident and emergency unit open or closed means life or death to a road accident victim in the future, but the maintenance of an underused accident and emergency unit could mean that the bill for the life of the accident victim is £100,000. Can we afford that life? Is it worth that much to us? If not, what is it worth? The necessity for facing up to the making of brutally overt choices like this can no longer be evaded in health services, and we as consumers owe it to the decision-makers to be aware of the pressures at work. As a society we have to reach a consensus on the values that we expect to affect these decisions, to demand sufficient information to make reasoned choices. No amount of extra funding for health will ever do away with the need to make these choices, rather it will bring with it the need to make more. Only one thing is certain, as Barbara Castle wrote in her introduction to the *Priorities* document in 1975, 'Choice is never easy, but choose we must.'[2]

What sort of choice are we talking about? Is it really possible to fling open a door of some hospital corridor and find an ashen-faced consultant, head in hands, saying to himself 'If I operate on Mr Jones this afternoon, that will cost the health service £5,000 which could be used to renovate the old people's ward at St Botolph's and thus bring a little sunshine into thirty old ladies' disadvantaged lives.' Or might he be saying to himself, 'I have four patients who need urgent treatment. There are only two beds available. Which of these patients will best repay the investment put into them by surgery and treatment, and which can society best afford to risk?'

'If I abandon or downgrade the patient with advanced cancer of the stomach in favour of two patients with hernias,' writes a doctor in the medical press, 'how do I make a cost benefit analysis? How do I equate the loss of six months' dyspepsia free survival with the economic utility of the return of two bread-winners to work?'

'An open heart operation in one of our teaching hospitals,' says a regional administrator, 'costs £28,000 and they do eight a week. Compare that to the service given to an old lady out in the country who's on a two-year waiting list to get a hearing-aid. So many people need them and they all need to be seen by a doctor first. So the doctor says, "What do I do, operate on this patient for cancer of the throat, or do I give the time to seeing the deaf old lady?" '

Public Expenditure on Health, a report of the Organization for Economic Cooperation and Development, recently pointed out that in the absence of rationing of health care by price, the only alternative is the rationing of health care by queuing, or the rationing of health care by the medical profession itself – a role for which doctors are not specifically trained and which they resent.[3] But despite the incessant flow of reports, recommendations and consultative documents, the planning committees and White Papers, doctors are the people who make the ultimate choices in rationing health. The public blames administrators for penny-pinching or for blocking progress, they blame politicians for theorizing and ignoring human needs, but the real, effective decision-makers in the health service are not administrators or politicians but the medical profession. At the latest estimate each consultant was responsible for the spending of a quarter of a million pounds each year, and each family doctor for the disposition of £36,000 in time and services. It is not a question of actually signing the cheques – if it were, doctors might be more cost-conscious – but of the ways in which doctors set in motion expensive trains of inquiry and treatment without consideration of the economic consequences.

'We doctors have it in our power to improve the situation,' writes a reproving doctor to his colleagues. 'We can stop admitting ambulant patients for investigation, diabetics for stabilizations, confine our admissions to emergencies and discharge patients as soon as they can be reasonably looked after at home, stop removing tonsils from children, do more day bed ops, use cheaper drugs, fewer antibiotics, stop referral on demand. It is we, not the public, who demand ten or so path. investigations on every patient to obtain a profile.' Not all doctors are as aware of the economic consequences of their actions as this one. The need to consider an overall budget is not something that is drummed into them at medical school. On the contrary, the consequences of the shelter offered by the National Health Service, and of their clinical freedom, has been to persuade them, however unconsciously, that they must do the best for each individual patient without counting the cost. The result is that in place of conscious rationing of health care, most doctors rely on a rationing mechanism familiar to us all – the waiting list.

The waiting list is the aspect of the NHS which attracts the most odium and the most bitter criticism from the public, but it replaces the rationing by capacity to pay which operates in other systems. When a resource is in short supply, be it a consultant, a GP, an X-ray machine or a hospital bed, that resource is best used by piling up the users so that no costly and wasteful gaps in its use occur. This is extremely distressing and sometimes even fatal for those who are piled up waiting, but it makes sense in terms of the rationing of a scarce commodity. Enoch Powell wrote in 1966:

If the hospital resources are to be continuously used, there must be a waiting list, a cistern from which a steady flow of cases can be maintained. Private practice can afford to have gaps because patients are buying time. Waiting lists ration demand for the more able, experienced or celebrated advice and treatment. Waiting lists are a status symbol. Like an iceberg, the significant part are the patients who aren't accepted or who have decided not to wait. At Christmas time or holidays it may be necessary to go far down a list to find a patient willing to come in. Trying to get waiting lists down is an activity about as helpful as trying to fill a sieve. Lists reproduce themselves effortlessly and automatically. They are a stable feature of the health service.[4]

So comparatively stable are waiting lists that their numbers have hovered steadily around the half-million mark ever since the health service began, despite fluctuations in population and repeated unsuccessful attempts to reduce them. Waiting lists for in-patient treatment peaked at over 600,000 in December 1976 but had dropped back below 600,000 in the spring of 1977. They are the visible symbol of postponed or evaded choices. If half a million people are asked to hold on, the chances are high that some will emigrate, some will get better all on their own, some will decide not to go through with treatment, some will die. Some will opt for the main advantage of private health care – swift service – and buy their way out of the queue. All these things happen at no further cost to the health service which can then concentrate its energies on those who stuck it out. Conscientious attempts to reduce waiting lists are not always rewarded by compliant behaviour from the public. A Birmingham hospital which made the attempt reported rather sourly to the medical journals that the effort may not have been worthwhile:

In this hospital, by steady pressure and extra work on the part of the medical and nursing staff, we have greatly reduced waiting time for appointments, for out patients and also for admission. Patients for admission, in almost all cases, are given a firm date for their admission which is nowhere near as far ahead as the figures suggested on a television programme. Since we have provided this improved service we have found that a steadily increasing number of patients default when their admission is due despite the fact that they are given a date and an opportunity to ask for an alternative. At times up to 40% of patients have failed to appear on the date arranged ... such behaviour of patients adds to the depression of morale in medical and nursing staff ... one is forced to ask whether the health service is so inadequate after all, or whether a vocal intellectual minority are demanding a higher quality and more expensive service than the populace at large desires or requires.

When conscious attempts to control an unconscious rationing device have such abortive results no wonder that doctors return to the old system. As former Minister of Health David Owen pointed out, 'It should not sound horrifying or cause alarm, if politicians and doctors admitted more freely that their decisions are often influenced, and even dominated, by the maxims of calculated neglect and masterly inactivity.'⁵ However, when pressures increase, the luxury of calculated neglect and evaded choice is no longer available. Someone has to sit down and make a conscious decision as to who shall have and who shall have not. The classic and often-quoted area of overtly exercised choice in medical treatment is the problem of kidney failure, a condition for which effective treatment exists, but still not enough of it. The treatment of kidney failure by dialysis (artificial cleansing of the blood through a machine), or by kidney transplant, is perhaps the most dramatic example of deliberate rationing in medicine. Of an estimated 7,000 kidney patients, the 35–40 kidney units in England and Wales have money and room to treat only a percentage. Decisions have to be taken as to the price of the life of each of these patients. Your chances of treatment are considerably lowered by age, whichever end of the spectrum you find yourself. In 1976, of 1,882 patients being treated, only 74 were children. If you contract kidney disease over the age of fifty-five your chances of treatment are likewise minimal. As one of the country's top kidney specialists said, 'the financial situation is now so acute that children are having to compete with adults for treatment and they tend to lose out because priority has to be given to adults who have families to look after and mortgages to maintain'. If the government were to provide enough trained personnel and equipment to treat everyone on purely medical grounds, the cost would be over £40 million.

But it isn't necessary to look at as specialized a field as kidney failure in order to find traumatic choices being made in the spending of money on health care. 'The example everyone always gives is of the kidney machine,' said a district administrator, 'but that's shroud-waving.' This particular administrator was recently faced with the specific task of cutting nearly half a million pounds off his £20 million budget. The district in question had been overspending and was faced with this kind of traumatic surgery as an emergency operation, but the kind of decision that the rationing entailed was common to every health district in the country on a day-to-day basis. There isn't enough money to meet the demands on the service being made by professional and public alike, so the service must resort to a continuous process of penny-pinching and balancing books. The main problem facing the financial administration is the open-ended commitment made for them by the individual doctor which makes it impossible for them to predict how much health care will be needed at any given time. The only way of saving money on health when the problem is treated in this *ad hoc* way is by cutting the service to the public. As one administrator explained:

The essence of the problem is trying to predict trouble spots. In the good old days you could buy your way out of trouble. Any fool can maintain equilibrium that way. I was trained in planning and development – i.e. in spending money – but now, if there isn't any money you have to get the equilibrium by taking a part out and rebalancing it that way. You can't buy your way out of trouble so you have to go back down the system and see what you can lose. The main problem is that commitment is determined by the way in which the doctor operates. He is not responsible for the follow-through therefore there is no advance estimate possible as to how much of anything you need. Everything that a doctor does commits the service to expenditure. When we were faced with the problem of cutting back, I said to the medical staff, 'You'll be committing the district to work but we can't support you. We have no back-up staff. There's not enough nurses, there's no physios, you can sing for secretaries.' Some fought back – there were a lot of hysterical letters, questions for M Ps and so on. They didn't want to be seen to be cutting back medical care, they didn't want to be seen to help us so they wouldn't advise us as to where cuts could be made. But this group got smaller in time. On the whole they agreed they were taking on too much work and they agreed that there would be no further development.

It was basically a question of too many patients for support staff to handle safely. We had to cancel open heart surgery because there were no staff for intensive care. We had to cancel a bed – an intensive care unit bed costs £30,000 a year in nursing staff alone with seven nurses to one bed. Nurses are normally about one-third of the pay-roll, so add on two-thirds – then since the pay-roll is about 80% of the total budget, add on another 20% and that bed works out at about £100,000 a year. A lot had to be done blind. Without some measure of medical care you're going to be horribly wrong sometimes. Switchboard operators, for example. You must have two in case one goes sick or something, and we only had one. We cut too fine on the nursing staff. We cut too fine on medical records staff and the level of errors went right up. We get 1,500 out patients a day in our biggest hospital and for each one the notes must be there waiting on the doctor's desk and they weren't. We cut too fine on physicists – the equipment started going on the blink through lack of maintenance. Then we didn't replace consultants who retired. By getting medical staff to look hard at the work they did it was possible not to replace, but you had to be careful because you could end up paying more in overtime to the doctors you had, than it would have cost you to pay the salary of an extra doctor. We've lost 580 jobs off the pay-roll in three years, but we haven't published that. The union shop stewards couldn't face up to it.

There are two major differences now. The proportion of staff pay-roll to the rest of the budget has crept up from 70 to 80%. It is easier to cut back on paper, paint, maintenance and brickwork. So the wards and offices look drab. Painting a waiting-room would cost £30, but you'd have to pay £4,000 a year for a painter on the pay-roll so it's not worth it. I think paint matters. There's no reason why the place should look scruffy, it hurts morale. We have a new hospital in the district where I live which is very pleasant and bright. It's had appalling staffing problems but the people like it because the public like a place to look crisp and efficient.

by dint of scraping and slaving away on a day-to-day basis, knocking problems on the head as they arise, the district has managed to keep spending down, but it still isn't down far enough. The rate of increase in work being done has dropped, but it hasn't actually reduced. Nobody is sure if this is because the doctors are working harder or better, or if the patients are benefiting or suffering because of the new pressures. The only remaining way to reduce the volume of work – in other words, the number of patients treated – is by closing down hospital beds, even closing hospitals. One obvious candidate in the district costs £4 million a year to run – money which, if saved, could be used to boost community health services, radiology and pathology departments in the other hospitals, and provide improved support services. But closing a hospital is a piece of radical surgery which the local community finds very hard to take. What no health service ever feels it can say to the public in these cases is that the hospital may already be run down to such a state that it is positively dangerous to health.

'Those patients who might have gone to X hospital may not be treated, but the hospital is very unsatisfactory because of the low numbers and calibre of its staff. A woman suffocated and died there recently while she was on a ventilator – this is what happens with organization in a hospital going downhill. Unless you put in a lot of money and staff it won't get better. Ideally, I would put in more consultant anaesthetists, more nursing cover, the lot, but if the country can't afford acute services run at that pitch then we should say "We'll do what we can do properly."

'If you let standards go you're on a slippery slope. The public is not aware of it. We haven't explained it to them.'

Since the economic crisis of the mid-seventies, resulting in across-the-board cuts in public spending, the scramble to save money on health services has become more frantic than it might otherwise have been, but the process of rationing health care has always gone on and always will go on. What the increased conflict between growing demand and limited supply is going to require in the future is a system of budgeting for health that is not based on backlogs of waiting patients, on panic-stricken sessions with the account books, on the *ad hoc* closure of expensive facilities because there is no money for staff. Those in charge of health services – and the public who use them – are going to have to face up to the need for a rational planning of resources according to a long-term national policy based on a much more critical look at the way in which money goes on health, and on a considered refereeing of the competition within the service. It is one of the more remarkable facts about the NHS that despite all the potential it offered for just this kind of rationality and long-term planning, it wasn't until 1975 – twenty-seven years after its foundation – that a British government made a conscious statement on the future priorities of the service. Even then, it seems unlikely that it would have done anything so cold-blooded if economic crisis and an acute shortage of cash had not made it imperative to look critically at the way the money was being spent. A growing awareness of profound inequalities in the service, lack of money for future plans, the visible limits on any expansion, combined with the immediate economic gloom, was the official acknowledgement that difficult direct choices could no longer be evaded. A third element lay behind the statement of priorities – the existence, since the managerial reorganization of the National Health Service in 1974, of a proper machinery for long-term planning and consultation. As one planner pointed out:

No one had ever said, 'what are the needs of the population for health care?' Planning, in peoples' minds in the past, always meant spending the extra 3%. No one ever looked at the existing resources and asked, 'Is the existing 100% of resource effective?' At present, planning is geared to input. The idea in the future is to gear it to outcome; to look at the ultimate objective. If you did this with mental health, for example, you would take into account good housing, income, recreation and so on – mental hospitals would come way down the list.

The *Priorities* document claims:

For the first time an attempt has been made to establish rational and systematic priorities in health care. There are two important aspects. One, the redistribution of resources in favour of deprived regions and areas; and second, encouragement of joint planning between health authorities and local authorities through the provision of special finance. Growth can only be afforded if cuts are made elsewhere. And we put people before buildings, so capital programmes are being cut.

In drawing up a consultative document on priorities, the government had in mind the problems that had arisen in the health service precisely through the lack of any such policy. Despite the existence of a National Health Service there is still what David Owen calls 'a general, remorseless trend towards inequality of care and provision – the inequalities of health care which still exist are the greatest challenge facing the National Health Service'. The responsibility for redressing the balance, which should have lain with the Department of Health and Social Security, has got lost in the day-to-day running of the cumbersome machinery which devotes its efforts to keeping things as they are. It is not simply a question of money since some sectors, maternity services, for example, have continued to chomp up money despite a falling birth-rate, while other sectors, such as provision for the mentally ill, have continued to fall behind. What a policy on priorities should be doing is reversing a phenomenon which works in the free flow of health care, and which was labelled by a British doctor who noted its operation in the industrial valleys of South Wales, as *The Inverse Care Law*.[6] The principle, which should be as familiar to every medical student as the twice times table once was to schoolchildren, states that the availability of good health care tends to vary inversely with the need for it in the population served – or, in simple words, if you need it, it isn't there. Dr Tudor Hart's much quoted essay points out that the law operates most fully when there is a free market in medical care, and that its effects are softened by some external, non-commercial control such as the National Health Service. Backward, isolated and under-privileged regions will continue to be so whatever the advances in the population at large; and in health care, as in so many other privileges, to those that hath shall it be given.

Within the NHS geographical inequalities show themselves at every level – between health regions, between areas and districts within those regions. At the last count, the region where most money was spent on health per head of population was the London-based region of North-East Thames at £90 per person per year. In Trent, the health region which covers an area of England from Yorkshire down to Leicestershire, each individual accounts for only £63 per year. But if you take the comparison down to district level the discrepancies vary even more wildly. Within North-East Thames the citizen of the London Borough of Camden accounts for £136 per annum, while the citizen of Essex only receives £50 worth of health care, even less than the supposedly disadvantaged citizen of Trent. Extra money has been allocated to certain regions which were obviously more deprived than the rest, but as somebody pointed out, it is very difficult to allow more money to be spent on facilities which simply don't exist in the first place. 'The difficulty,' explained a spokesman from Trent, 'is to show what you haven't got. You can really only show deprivation in terms of figures. Per capita we have the fewest beds, the fewest doctors, the fewest nurses, the fewest G Ps, the longest waiting lists and the largest G P lists. North-West Derbyshire district is probably the worst off. It's very isolated country in the Peak district and the facilities simply don't exist.'

As Alice in Wonderland would have been quick to point out, you can really only have more if you've got something already. The greatest imbalances which have resulted from the unconscious rationing at work in health services are between the urban and rural areas, an imbalance which is being further exaggerated by the decline of other rural services such as transport. This means that someone who wants to visit the nearest G P surgery or hospital out patients' clinic, or see a friend in hospital, may have impossible journeys to make, or at least long waits for bus connections, or indeed have to walk. The National Federation of Women's Institutes conducted a nationwide survey of rural health services as their evidence to the Royal Commission on the National Health Service, and they came up with some alarming facts.[7] Quite apart from the ruin of the public transport system in the countryside, and the isolation of villages and households that has followed, they found that over half the settlements they surveyed had no doctor's surgery, 89% had no optician, 84% had no dentist who would accept National Health patients. 75% were without a chemist, and where there were rural pharmacies many of them are threatened with closure. As a result, a trip to the nearest hospital might mean a round journey of eighty miles with difficult bus connections.

The priorities put forward for consultation by the government threw light on these neglected areas of the service, and on the way inequalities had evolved between specialities as well as regions. They put greater emphasis on primary care, on community services, on looking after the increasing population of old people. They acknowledged the third-class service being given to the mentally ill and handicapped, and long-stay patients. They pointed out that as the money for improving community and primary care had to come from somewhere, it would come from the acute and hospital services. Within the acute services it nodded to the need to reduce waiting times and to narrow geographical gaps. It pointed out the need to examine certain commonly used medical procedures with a more critical eye for cost-effectiveness. The document consequently drew gasps of pain from what might be called the medical establishment. The *British Medical Journal* pointed out that Mrs Castle, in placing people before buildings, was bowing to public sentiment and allowing her heart to rule her head. A less guarded view was expressed by the member of the Royal College of Physicians who told an area administrator that *Priorities* was a 'pernicious document'. For all its basic common sense and the truth of the needs which it pointed out, the inhabitants of the centres of medical excellence regarded the *Priorities* document as a besieging force come to take the bastions of true medicine. By all means help old ladies and mental defectives; by all means put resources into stopping people smoking, but don't do it at the expense of acute medicine where the real business is carried out.

It is very early days yet for a conscious system of rationing health care according to pre-determined priorities to have taken root, but given the growing pressures on health services, it is an idea with which both professionals and public are going to have to live. Maybe one reason for its long postponement has been the distastefulness with which many of us regard the need to make what are emotional and moral, as much as economic, choices. Underlying any statement of priorities involving money and health is the fundamental question – how much is a human life worth? It is a question already answered on an *ad hoc* basis every day in the health service, but at the cost of wild discrepancies. The life of a man who contracted a rare tropical disease proved to be worth half a million pounds. A study in the *New England Journal of Medicine* worked out that the cost of a case of cancer detected by the end of a series of six tests endorsed by the American Cancer Society was $47 million.[8] In any health system, the maintenance of a million-dollar life is only upheld at the expense of a number of cheaper ones. A recent discussion of the problem in the *British Medical Journal* pointed out that 'as the health service implicitly places certain values on life already, a means of making this valuation more rational and explicit can only improve the quality and quantity of health care ... Even if extra resources were to be made available to the health service, choices would still have to be made against a background of some needs being unmet.'[9] It pointed out that the implicit value of a human life in different instances – as calculated by safety measures taken in building, a screening measure on pregnant women, the introduction of safety cabs on tractors and the withdrawing of child-proofed drug containers – varied between £50 per life saved and £20 million. Some rationally arrived-at baseline is needed if health services are to be delivered with any justice to the population, and the public could and should participate by shouldering at least part of the decision as to how much risk is acceptable to them. If any conscious rationing of health care is to be successful, and if there is to be any equality in the provision of health services to a nationwide community, then the public must enter the debate through the channels – such as Community Health Councils and the press – that are available to it. More money is not the simple answer. We ourselves can no longer avoid making some kind of decision on the value of life and its quality.

3 Doctor Power

In the absence of strong direction from any other quarter we have traditionally allowed the health service to be shaped for us by its most dominant professional group, the doctors. The general public, that pool of taxpayers and potential patients, suffers from the common misapprehension that the NHS was set up for its benefit, and is run in order to foster its well-being. Much of the disappointment and frustration that we feel with the apparent inadequacies and inequalities of the health service spring from this simple belief. How much more comprehensible would the ways of the health service be if we accepted the truth of the matter; that the health service, like any other enormous bureaucracy with such limitless demands made upon it, is run by the professionals involved in their own interests. No other group in the health service, despite the growing power of administrators and planners, has had a stronger influence on the shape of the service than the medical profession. And yet we seem to have ended up with a service which satisfies neither the doctors nor the patients. One reason for this is the most fundamental dilemma facing any health service – the fact that the interests of medicine and the interests of a health service are not one and the same. All the ethics, traditions and practice of medicine are based on the individual commitment of one doctor to one patient. All the ideals, promises and projections of a health service are based on an equitable and accessible service to a population. This is the congenital deformity with which each health service is born, that a universal service has to be based upon an unbreachable personal commitment.

In order to understand the nature of this commitment and its effect on the moulding of the service, it is necessary to look more closely at the doctor's training, at his role, and at its rock and foundation, the concept of clinical freedom. Before any organized health system exists there are doctors. The history of the health service, as opposed to the history of medicine, is the history of their struggles with politicians and bureaucrats to keep things running the way they see fit, and from the inception of the NHS to the present day, the history of the medical profession within the health service has been one of continuing effort to maintain both an unchallenged professional freedom, and the powerful and privileged voice that goes with it. Out of the near million workers in the NHS, only 77,000 are doctors, a proportion of one doctor to approximately 800 people in the population at large. Their importance is out of all proportion to their numbers. Whether they are GPs in a small country community, or consultants in a busy teaching hospital, they have traditionally represented authority and have enjoyed a unique respect and prestige and, as a consequence, a certain self-confidence. Unfortunately for its members, the future of the profession looks increasingly uncomfortable. Its autonomy is being threatened from every quarter – by the increasing militancy and self-assertion of all the other workers in the health service, by the economic pressures which limit the kind of medicine they can afford to practise, by a less compliant public who are more likely to question the doctor's traditional authoritarianism, by the rocketing complexity of medical procedures and chemotherapies which have put an end to the pretence of omniscience and have brought in an urgent need for evaluation in health care. Assaulted from all these fronts, the medical profession is operating increasingly on the defensive.

In the past the physician, whether witch-doctor, priest, folk-healer or quack, traditionally held a special position of power and responsibility in the community. In the best of systems this authority is exercised with the strongest sense of responsibility. The Hippocratic oath, the first expressed outline of a physician's role in society, is little more than a list of trusts and restrictions. The doctor accepts the responsibility to keep his oath, to pass on his knowledge of healing without charge.

I will follow that system or regimen which according to my ability and judgement I consider for the benefit of my patients and abstain from whatever is deleterious and mischievous. I will give no deadly medicine to anyone if asked, nor suggest any such counsel. Nor will I aid a woman to procure an abortion. With purity and holiness I will pass my life and practise my art ... into whatever houses I enter, I will go there for the benefit of the sick and will abstain from every act of mischief and corruption, and above all from seduction. Whatever in my professional practice – or even not in connection with it – I see or hear in the lives of men that ought not to be spoken of abroad, I will not divulge, deeming that in such matters, we should be silent. While I keep this oath unviolated may it be granted to me to enjoy life and the practice of my art, always respected among men, but should I break or violate this oath, may the reverse be my lot.

Much of this is now out of date. The procuring of abortion is a commonplace. The giving of deadly medicines, or at least the withholding of life-prolonging ones, more common than admitted. Purity and holiness are no longer valued virtues, and the directly religious aspects of medical care are much rarer than they used to be. Science has replaced God. Professional competence is more important than religious duty. The doctor who knows what is good for him still abstains from seduction of his patients, but society is more tolerant of sexual peccadilloes than it once was. Doctors are, after all, only human. But by being only human they lose a great deal of the homage that was due to the doctor-priest. With the acceptance of these trusts, and the assumption of these special responsibilities, goes a unique respect which can still be enjoyed on the hospital ward or in the GP's surgery. Doctors who have joined the civilian branches, so to speak, leaving the front line for the administration of public health or the laboratory, freely admit that they miss the gratitude of patients, the deference of nurses, the unquestioned value put upon them by everyone with whom they come into contact. It may be nonsense, it may not be good for them, it may encourage them to play God and lose the common touch, but it's fun.

The natural reverse of this coin is that where doctors are seen to break the codes, to reveal themselves as all too human, they are subject to a special odium. In any society where money is at the heart of the exchange between doctor and patient, the quickest way to earn this disrespect is to be seen to be greedy and corrupt. Maybe one reason for the mounting rate of lawsuits in the United States, and the consequently crippling rate of malpractice insurance, is that doctors are seen to be so commercially minded and well rewarded. The people who sue them are simply repaying one kind of rapaciousness with another. The doctor who makes undue profit is quite openly enriching himself out of the misfortunes of other people. In the past it could have been by selling a fraudulent elixir of life or the secret of eternal youth. Nowadays it is just as likely to be an unnecessary and potentially dangerous operation, an expensive and useless course of treatment. Where profit is directly allied to medicine the doctor needn't be surprised if his traditional purity and holiness comes under suspicion.

Even in societies like Britain where the doctor is paid either directly, or indirectly, by the state, his increasing preoccupation with money is undermining his traditional authority. Where doctors can descend to using the same industrial disputes and wage structure as any other worker in the health service, then the rest of us can see that self-interest is just as strong a motivation with the healing class as with the hospital porter. Doctors in Britain may not descend to the brand of blatant commercialism that caused an American doctor to rip fifteen stitches out of a boy's hand because he didn't have the money to pay for them, but they have declared themselves ready to desert patients in order to press pay claims, and by abdicating, however briefly, their special responsibility for the patient, they also abdicate their rights to the special respect which is one of the invisible perks of the job. Perhaps even more significantly they make their own contribution to the weakening of the central importance of that relationship.

Doctors within their own society, reinforced by the traditions of the Royal Colleges and the medical schools, may place a high value on professional qualifications, on technical and scientific ability, on the number of papers written and exams passed.

Most patients place a higher value on human qualities. As long
as a doctor is not proved to be an incompetent idiot, the kind of
man who chops off the wrong leg or prescribes drugs which
make them worse, most people reserve their respect and affection for the sympathetic and approachable doctor: the doctor
who treats them as a human being and not a moron; the
doctor who bothers to explain what he is about. A great many
doctors like to pretend that if it weren't for the restrictions of
the NHS this is the kind of doctor they would all be, but it is
more a matter of temperament than time. Sympathy and communication can be established just as well in five minutes as in
fifteen, and studies of communication between doctor and
patient show that satisfaction depends far more on the attitude
of the doctor than on the time he spends or the treatment he
prescribes. A report based on 800 different hospital consultations in California not only found no correlation whatsoever between the length of time the doctor spent with the
patient and the patient's satifaction, but did find a direct statistical correlation between the patient's satisfaction and the
amount of purely sociable conversation between the two. A
salutory experience which bears this out is told by a young
houseman about a close shave in the casualty department. It
was he, in the chain of treatment and diagnosis, who was actually responsible for missing a fractured dislocation of the hip
and sending the patient home overnight. When the patient re-
turned to hospital in great pain and suffering the added com-
plication of pneumonia, he set about accusing everyone in the
hospital of negligence – except the young houseman who, he
said, was the only one of the lot of them who had treated him
like a human being.

The health service, by and large, has been run according to
what doctors rather than the public think is good medicine and
good doctoring, but this balance is shifting slightly. We are
more questioning and doctors are no longer so sure. They are
suffering from a severe crisis of self-confidence. As the range of
what medicine can do expands, and the range of what it is asked
to do expands equally, though not always in the same direction,

more and more people within the medical profession are won-
dering exactly what they are there for. Until the new social and
economic forces began to encroach on the traditional preserves
of the medical profession, the doctor probably had a much
clearer idea of who he was and what he had to do and how to go
about it. Now, as the Royal College of Physicians phrased it in
its evidence to the Royal Commission on the National Health
Service, 'morale is low ... there is a feeling that an un-
trammelled relationship between doctor and patient is becoming increasingly difficult to maintain and that the individual
patient no longer occupies the central position that he or she
must occupy if the service is to have meaning.' The problem as
phrased by a medical management expert is 'of getting the service people to a sense of market values, of getting a caring
profession to understand that what they do may not be the most
important thing in the world. A doctor brought up in a traditional medical school on the Hippocratic oath may not understand that other things have some value too.'

But is it a doctor's job to see his insignificance in the scheme
of things? A sense of market values, an instinct for business
efficiency, a cost-effective approach to his own patients are the
last things that the average doctor wants to develop, or that the
individual patient wants his doctor to have. Just as medical
interests conflict with health service interests, so do our interests
as taxpayers and as patients conflict. As taxpayers we should be
all for evaluation, rationalization and streamlining of the health
service. As potential patients we want all the bias, emotional
blackmail and partisanship that can be urged in our favour.
We want our doctor to think we are the most important problem in the world, we want him to fight to the last ditch for every
ounce of clinical freedom he needs to treat us to the very best,
and medical tradition, despite all the inroads into its authority,
is still on our side. The doctor still sees himself as the champion
of the individual patient, tilting his lance at the army of grey
men in defence of his own particular patch of human rights.

The self-image of the doctor is formed at medical school and
is something, like the secret of brown sauce, that is passed on,

unadulterated, from generation to generation. The prestigious consultant who trails students behind him on a ward-round in the teaching hospital is instilling into his students the desire (in most cases) to wear a white coat and trail students in their turn. They pick up the mythology of the profession. They are taught that clinical freedom of the individual doctor to treat the individual patient to what he considers the best is at the root of all medicine, and that any interference with this principle is interference with a divine right and leads to the downfall of medicine as we know it. Not for nothing did Michael Foot, in his biography of Aneurin Bevan, write that 'much of the strongest bent in the medical mind was a non-political conservatism, a revulsion against all change, a habit of intellectual isolation which enabled them to magnify any proposal for reform into a totalitarian nightmare'. The attitude is much the same today. The NHS remains a great concession made by the medical profession to the nation, and a privilege which, if we persist in interfering, they might be forced to withdraw at any time. Politicians are as much the natural enemies of doctors as foxes are of rabbits, and they have been joined by the growing number of administrators. These attitudes, which are entirely comprehensible in an older generation of a naturally conservative profession, are being successfully passed on to the younger branches. A young medical student of normally radical views was asked what she was being taught in medical school about the way in which the health service worked and she said, without a second's hesitation, 'Well, we know that administrators are the enemy and we have to do everything we can to fight them.' She was no more aware of the wider social and economic issues that shape the health service than the stuffiest out-of-date consultant from the darkest corner of a Royal College.

School-leavers apply to medical school in large numbers – at Edinburgh, for example, there were recently 2,000 applications for 150 places – and they apply for barely articulated reasons. Over 20% will come from medical families, something which is attacked as nepotism, on the one hand, and defended on the other with the argument that at least they will know the irregularities and demands of the job at first hand. A group of young students interviewed on the radio gave every reason from job security to the fact that, when they played doctors and nurses as children, it was the nurses who got bossed around while the doctors had all the fun. One student will choose medicine because he got good results in science exams at school and has the sheer technical ability needed. Another will be attracted by the human contact. They are unlikely, in Britain, to be drawn by the dazzling financial prospects that attract doctors in other countries. Surveys have shown that a student's idea of what a job in medicine involves are very hazy. They expect high status in the community, good social position. People at school may have impressed upon them the high security of a doctor's job but they are unlikely to realize what the job entails in day-to-day tasks.

Medical schools can take the *crème de la crème* academically. They demand, and get, the best school examination results. As a consequence they get academically bright students. Whether these students make the best doctors is a different question entirely. The average patient likes to think that he will meet with human understanding from a doctor but it is surprisingly common to meet doctors whose competence at simply getting on with people, at establishing an easy relationship with their patients, is staggeringly low, whatever their A-level results. We've all met the hospital doctor who doesn't bother to introduce himself or ask if he can prod you, the GP who asks what the trouble is and looks at the floor or the ceiling as if that could provide the answer. Apart from those students who already have doctors in the family, the rest of them will have no clearer idea what a doctor is or does than the rest of us. They are fed with the same films, the same books, the same image of the doctor that appears in the media. They will probably think that the doctor's job is the diagnosis and treatment of illness, that illness is cured by treatment, and that this is what health care is about, a concept that is true so far as it goes, which isn't very far. What a student then goes on to learn in medical school, the self-image of the doctor that is created in him, the concept of what medicine is *for*, will shape for ever the way in which he expects to work, and in consequence, the way in which his country's health services operate. In countries where doctors have largely been trained in Western hospital medicine but whose own countries are actually beset by problems of basic public health and rural medicine, the results of this totally inappropriate training can be disastrous. But even within the highly scientific Western system of medicine, what a doctor learns can be equally inappropriate to the world outside the walls of the teaching hospital, with results as depressing for the doctor as for his potential patients. Patterns of dissatisfaction are laid down which may never be broken.

In many ways the five or six years' basic training which a doctor receives at a cost of over £30,000 to the rest of us, largely fail to reflect the needs of the society which he will be going out to serve. Doctors are trained to deal with abnormalities, with acute conditions, with crises and rarities. They are trained almost entirely on patients who are presented to them in hospital, and not even in the average district general hospital, but in the more specialized surroundings of the teaching hospital which has carried out a further selection from the nation's pool of patients, and concentrates even more highly on the difficult and rare cases. 90% of illness occurs, and is dealt with, in the community, but the average medical student will be protected from this mundane collection of coughs, colds and backaches. He will also be protected from the handicapped, the old, the social problems that make up the bulk of the general practitioner's work; the material on which he is trained represents the specialized interests of the specialized group of people who teach him – the technical problems, the fascinating obscurities, the patients who offer most scope for tests and probes.

Professor Thomas McKeown points out, rather cynically, in his book *The Role of Medicine*, that there is an inverse relationship between the interest of a disease to the doctor, and the use of the treatment to the patient, and that the mechanistic, technological approach of modern medicine has led to the neglect of the vast majority of sick people who offer little scope for it. 'Acute hospitals,' he says, 'are becoming more selective, teaching hospitals even more so, so training will be done in places even more remote from most health problems.'[1]

It is not surprising if the interests of the teachers and their ideas of what medicine is about, rub off on the students. The newer medical schools in Britain, in Southampton, Leicester, Nottingham, have a higher component of social medicine, a greater awareness of what the average GP needs to know, rather than a mission to train future neuro-surgeons, but most schools carry on the old traditions. 'The young chaps are more socially aware,' said a doctor, 'places like Nottingham and Southampton have a different approach, but at places like Barts they'll be training them in the traditional way with the chap in the white coat who trails them through the ward and humiliates the patients. Medical education is far from right. If you wanted to teach doctors you should ask the basic question – what do they *do*?'

'It is essential to find a new kind of student,' says a radical GP, 'and therefore a new kind of doctor. We should help our students to become doctors of a different kind from their teachers. It is a doctor's job to become the person most enthusiastic and knowledgeable about health in the community, to do an anticipatory and continuous style of preventive work rather than the discontinuous, sympto-response, emergency type of work which is more fashionable.'

A correspondent to the *British Medical Journal* points out the dilemma of the medical schools, that the teaching hospitals fill their wards with patients suffering from obscure disorders simply to satisfy the jaded palates of the specialists who work there, while the great majority of hospital patients throughout the country suffer from degenerative disorders, or simply the complications of old age. Because of the engineering approach to medicine, social and behavioural factors take second place, and so do all those of us who aren't immediately or easily curable. Not many students are trained, as McKeown trained himself, to wonder at the patient's bedside whether the hospital was making anyone any wiser or better. 'I soon came to the conclusion,' he writes, 'that most of the time we were not.'

Failure to consider the patient as a whole person with a mind and a social background results in the kind of impersonality in medicine most detested and complained of by patients. Few patients bear a grudge if a treatment is not as successful as it might be, as long as an honest and sympathetic effort has been made. Nearly all of us resent being treated as a number, a mindless complaint, 'the liver in bed three', a mild nuisance without whom the system would run a great deal more efficiently. A medical student goes through months and months of theory before he or she actually faces a patient. Most teaching time is taken up with physics, chemistry, anatomy, microbiology, physiology. What students are not taught is more significant. The recommendations of *The Royal Commission on Medical Education*[2] that departments of community medicine should be established in medical schools, took over ten years to implement. Out of twenty-five medical schools, only seven gave six or more hours of teaching on occupational medicine and ten of them didn't teach it at all. Historically the reason for this concentration on acute medicine at the expense of primary care, occupational medicine and attention given to the long-term, is the growth of medical education inside the system of voluntary hospitals. Voluntary hospitals concentrated deliberately on the short-term, curable patient. Schools grew up within them and that was the teaching material. The teachers were the consultants of the hospitals and so the system perpetuated and perpetuates itself. Medical students, like any others, want to do what they have been taught to do, sometimes with a distorting effect on service to the community as a whole.

One great complaint which rises from those doctors who are preparing to emigrate (whether from Britain, or Bangladesh, or the Philippines) to some rosier clime where doctors practise as they please and get well paid for it, is that they can no longer practise real medicine. What do they mean? What is real medicine? Real medicine is presumably what they think they have been taught to practise, but if it is something that doesn't exist outside the teaching hospital then it is not real medicine at all, and the teaching hospital is failing utterly in its job of providing doctors to serve a community. Doctors are not being taught to do what they have to do. They are being trained in and for ideal conditions that simply don't exist. If they find that they have to go abroad to practise, then there is a huge gap in expectation between the real world and the world in which they have been taught. 'Doctors,' says one theory, 'study medicine which they don't practise, and practise social science which they have not studied.' If discontent in the health service is to be reduced, then here is a root cause which must be tackled.

It is being increasingly recognized that the expectations set up by traditional medical education form one of the most fundamental causes of the discontents within the health services today. In recent years the problem has come under close scrutiny, and the setting up of new medical schools has enforced a fresh look at the old curriculum with the result that the newer schools have a higher component of community studies, and a stronger sense of medicine as part of the social services and not simply a separate field of technical activity. But even this may not be enough to ensure that medicine and its practitioners in the future are trained with the kind of perspective and social awareness that will produce an equitable and caring health service, and not simply pockets of good medicine. The Labour Party, in its evidence to the Royal Commission, made some very specific suggestions as to how the medical profession in future could widen its horizons through a change in the bias of medical education. It suggested that all potential medical students should spend a preliminary year working in the NHS in some unskilled capacity in order to get a worm's eye view of the problems that lie ahead. It suggested that there should be some element of common training with other students in related professions within the health service, such as nursing, social work and administration, so that the elitism that is inevitably built into the medical student can be contained by the business of seeing the needs of other groups within the service and the importance of teamwork. Their horizons would also be widened by seeing the different approaches of different workers to the problems of providing health for the community. The manifesto states that:

It makes a nonsense of the so-called integrated organization of the NHS for clinical doctors, who authorize the bulk of its resources, to have a narrow view of health care and continue to act as competing soloists, pushing their claims for the most technically advanced plant and equipment, rather than working with other professional groups on how best to allocate limited resources to meet all health needs, including those for prevention and care.[3]

And in principle, the British Medical Association agrees. Pointing out that multi-disciplinary health teams are now basic to patient care, it confirms that medical education should go much further than it does at present to give a future doctor a proper understanding of what other disciplines can do. Despite this across-the-board agreement on future needs in medical education, performance is more difficult to come by than promise. As we have seen, the earlier recommendations of the *Todd Report on Medical Education,* for increased teaching of community and occupational medicine, general practice, mental illness and so on, have not been acted upon in many places, particularly London, and continuing pressure is obviously needed in order to change the course of an education that has trundled along the same lines for many years. However, the pressure is not lacking. The British Medical Association underlines the need for the training of young doctors to take place in a less rarefied atmosphere than that provided by some teaching hospitals, and suggests that in future, students should be attached to district general hospitals for part of their training to get a more realistic view of the problems they might face in the future. In a developed country like Britain, the distorting effects of the teaching hospital on the health service, although noticeable, are more excusable than they are in a developing country where they drain money and talent like a black hole, and leave nothing but dissatisfied doctors who are competent in a kind of medicine they can't practise without going abroad. A student in an African teaching hospital was asked how he would determine how far advanced in pregnancy a woman might be – this in a country where only 15% of the population have any contact with any level of medical services. He said he would use an ultrasonic scanner. What service does any country do for itself by producing medical practitioners so utterly unprepared for reality? And for whose benefit and interest are students being trained? If it is not for the community in which they are to serve, then it can only be for some ideal world of medicine that only exists within the profession itself.

Having spent some of the most impressionable years of their lives in the teaching hospital it is no wonder that many doctors find the outside world traumatic. They have come to see the abnormal as normal. They have come to see the rest of the inhabitants of the hospital as deferential supplicants, tea-makers and errand-runners, or unnerved patients devoid of their usual resilience and bounce. Life is not a teaching hospital, nor is the NHS simply a laboratory for interesting conditions. Nor, where it is a laboratory, is it even a spectacularly well-equipped one. Where a young doctor might have become used to the best of what medicine has to offer, he has to go out and make do within the limitations of a health service funded by a society which, in itself, is increasingly in the business of simply making do. The fortunate few who get the latest medical toys to play with are outnumbered by the vast numbers of doctors who have to practise medicine in conditions of endurance and improvisation. No wonder that they feel rather wistfully that the aura of prestige and authority that touched them like gold-dust in the medical school, has no more substance in later life than Wordsworth's clouds of glory. As medical prestige declines from the glorious promise of the teaching hospital, too many doctor's lives are but a sleep and a forgetting. Nor is this decline in medical prestige confined to Britain. A survey of world-wide health services reports a diminution almost everywhere of doctor power and a decline in the sway of medical associations. The mood of the times is against unchallenged authoritarianism, and the inherent individualism of doctors is struggling to survive in the need to rationalize health services. Gone are the days recalled by a psychiatrist when the medical superintendent of a hospital was God. 'His power has been whittled away bit by bit with the rise of other professions, notably by administrators, by nurses, by other colleagues. In the old days, when a doctor came into the room everyone automatically stood up. There was more of a family-type structure in a hospital then so there was some case for saying they needed a father figure. With them we have lost a structure of authority and accountability that is missing today. Nowadays so many people have a voice you don't know what the hell is going on.'

Father figures, witch-doctors, priest-physicians only obtain their power by virtue of collusion with the rest of us. Like fairies, if we believe in them, they twinkle and flourish. If we withdraw our faith they wither and fade away. Slowly we are all becoming more questioning of what is done to us in the name of medicine, of the way in which the health service is run, above all of the divine right of the medical profession to dispose of health services in the way they see fit without explaining themselves to us or to each other. We will never have a health service that functions as well as it might while the central profession involved in its decision-making is chosen and trained to ignore the needs of society as a whole, and the ambitions and ideals of its colleagues in other professions.

4 The Holes in the Net

The traditional search for individual excellence in medicine and the bias of the teaching hospitals towards highly specialized acute medicine, lead to large areas of neglect in the health service. Not only do these betray the fundamental principles of medicine, since the one-to-one relationship is necessarily affected in these areas, but they betray the original promise of the NHS to provide equality of access for all to the best of medical care. The way in which doctors choose to work has a very profound effect on the distribution and quality of health services. They can concentrate themselves into areas in which they may not be strictly needed. They can be noticeably absent from the areas where they are needed. By giving their services to the few they can deny them to the many, and they ensure that the Inverse Care Law can be seen to operate with great clarity within medicine itself. Five million people present themselves to their GPs each year with a mental health problem. Over 14% of the population is aged over sixty-five and it uses up to 70% of all hospital beds, but mental health and geriatric services are the two areas of medicine with the lowest prestige and which have the most difficulty in attracting any kind of resource, whether high-quality staff, buildings or money.

It would be extremely unfair to blame the medical profession individually and entirely for this state of affairs. The inheritance of old and derelict hospitals, the ambivalence of social attitudes towards the old and abnormal have a profound effect on the 'caring' services, but the effects of medical education and traditional ambitions in the medical profession have done nothing whatsoever to rescue these services from their slough of despond. The concentration of medicine on cure rather than care has led to the existence of medical slums. The interest of the bulk of the medical profession has always been in those patients for whom they feel something can be done, a cure effected. The rest of those people who might reasonably claim to be in ill health, but for whom there is no hope of immediate cure, are treated as second-, even third-class citizens. 'There is no prestige,' says the doctor cynically, 'in looking after mad old ladies.' The neglect demonstrates itself at every level, in sheets of financial statistics, in staffing ratios, in the lack of enthusiasm of medical school graduates to work in these areas. It demonstrates itself most of all in the outward show, in the old buildings, the isolation and the tangible air of apathy that is to be found in the worst long-stay institutions. We have inherited more than the outward shell of nineteenth-century attitudes towards the poor, mad and destitute – the workhouse and asylums. We have inherited the stigma, the suppressed disapproval and fear of those who depend on us without returning our costly investment by being lovable, endearing, responsive, curable or rewarding in any way.

Dependent old people can be time-consuming, difficult, unclean and infuriating. So can the mentally ill and handicapped. They are discouraging sights to put before the bright-eyed young medical students who want to learn how to cure people, so the bright-eyed young medical student is unlikely to come across them. Is it at all surprising that when new medical graduates leave the teaching hospital, they have no intention of working in the slums of the health service, or that, as a consequence, the slums are not razed and rebuilt? Any survey of career preferences among young doctors is a clear indication of the priorities of the medical profession within the health service. The hospital specialities of general medicine, surgery, obstetrics draw by far the highest number of entrants and, in some lists, specialities like geriatrics and mental handicap are noticably absent. They are swallowed up in the anonymity of 'other choices'. The curriculum of medical schools is greatly to blame, as we have seen, in simply ignoring the 'care' areas of medicine, but the imbalance that starts at medical school is exaggerated by the way other career incentives work. The greatest of these is the merit award system.

The merit award system is one of the most archaic aspects of the extraordinary mish-mash of compromise that keeps the British medical profession operating within a state health system. Consultants are currently paid salaries on a scale between £7,000 plus and £10,000. This far from extravagant range of payments for Britain's top doctors is augmented – secretly and anonymously – by a system of government-distributed 'merit award' payments, sums ranging from a couple of thousand pounds a year to an extra ten thousand pounds. They are distributed according to a sliding scale to those doctors whom colleagues agree are worthy to receive them. Nobody theoretically knows who gets them, at least not by name. But certain aspects of the merit award system are well known, such as the fact that they are very unevenly distributed among the different branches of medicine and that this distribution only serves to exaggerate the inequalities that already exist. To the glamorous appeal of the highly technical, life and death specialities, such as heart surgery, is added the much higher likelihood of being much better paid. 71·4% of theoracic surgeons receive a merit award. 63·4% of neurosurgery consultants and 68·9% of cardiologists. But only 12·5% of consultants in community medicine are so lucky, only 24·9% of consultants in mental health, or 24·7% of consultants in rheumatology and rehabilitation. The rather grim aura that hangs about long-stay patients and the chronic sick or handicapped is not dispelled by the fact that doctors who work with them will not even be well rewarded for it.

The pull of the financial attractions of merit awards is compounded by the further financial incentives of private practice. The pickings from private practice in geriatrics or mental handicap are nil. The money that can be made from a private practice in obstetrics or heart surgery is very handsome indeed. Of over 12,000 consultants in England and Wales, half are part-time, which means that they have the opportunity of undertaking private practice as well as their NHS commitments. The part-timers tend to work in the lucrative, marketable areas of medicine. The full-timers are to be found in those areas which offer the least chance of private work. All these considerations have a visibly adverse effect on the distribution of doctors throughout the service. One estimate says that the national average for the mentally handicapped is one consultant per 400 patients. In the more prestigious areas of acute medicine the proportion can be as high as one consultant to 30 patients. In one district in the Home Counties there is one single-handed geriatrician among the 70 or so consultants of whom 20 are in general medicine and 30 in surgery. The junior staff, too, are concentrated heavily on the side of acute medicine. Doctors talk gloomily about a future over-supply of medical graduates, but as long as the distribution of medical manpower concentrates so heavily in some areas and leaves others so bereft of attention, there will be no shortage of work for future doctors to do.

The NHS is well aware of the imbalance in the service it offers the public, and since 1976 the official priority areas have been old people, the mentally ill and handicapped, the chronically sick and the physically handicapped. It is officially recognized that the people in these very large categories have been shamefully neglected in health service terms, and the government, along with the people who work with these patients, would like to see more attention paid, more money invested, better staff, better buildings and more community support provided. The theoreticians say how splendid it is that the government is putting more emphasis on the down-and-outs of the health service. The people who are actually involved laugh sardonically. They've heard it all before. If they care about their patients they've already been fighting for improvements for years and have become tired and cynical. If they don't care about their patients, then they probably started out tired and cynical and nothing will change for them. Geriatricians tending old people in outdated almshouses watch their numerous colleagues in acute medicine win battles for whatever extra cash may be going. Consultants in mental handicap harden into cynicism as they read yet another public commitment to their patients that isn't followed by any public money. Psychiatrists working from overcrowded nineteenth-century warehouses of the sick and inadequate wonder when pious statements about community care are ever going to be fulfilled.

The divisions between acute medicine and long-term care have their roots deep in nineteenth-century social attitudes and nineteenth-century hospitals. There is, in the visible chasm between them, a legacy of attitudes from the days when to be old and destitute was almost a punishable offence. Curable conditions concentrated in the voluntary hospitals, but madness, destitution and senility put one beyond the pale of medical interests. The attitudes linger on, both among the general public and within the medical profession, and the inequalities that result reveal themselves in rather startling figures. In 1973, a bed-week for the mentally handicapped cost £28·02, less than it costs to keep a man in prison. Expenditure per patient week for nursing in mental hospitals is 46% that of acute hospitals, the cost of doctors only 26% and the total costs – including food and upkeep of surroundings – only 34%. A shortage of medical care is one thing, but why does it cost so much less to feed a long-stay patient than a patient in an ordinary hospital? The problems of the old and the mentally ill and handicapped are not at all minor ones, so it's worth a closer look at why, when medical responsibility and social attitudes become confused, the result is often appalling neglect.

I. The Land Where the Crumblies Live

The greatest social problem confronting any Western country today is the growing age of its population. In England alone there are more than 6·5 million people aged over sixty-five – 14% of the total population – and the number is growing each year. By 1980 nearly 15% of the population will be over sixty-five and by the turn of the century, over 1% of the population will be over eighty-five.[1] In certain areas where old people like to retire and look backwards over life, the percentage of old people in the local community is much higher. Walk along the sea-front in any well-favoured seaside resort and count them. There is more than one seaside town in Britain which is known unkindly as Costa Geriatrica, and in the balmy south-west of the country, for example, the proportion of old people is nearing 20%. The problem facing any Minister of Health is that any increase he can squeeze in his annual budget will certainly be swallowed up by the infirmities and dependence of this ageing population. By 1992, says one calculation, 93·7 of non-maternity beds for women and 73·5% of hospital beds for men will be filled with old age pensioners.

There are two aspects to this growing problem. One is that there are simply more old people around than there used to be. The other is that as people avoid the hazards of childhood, youth and middle age and cruise sagely towards the harbour of old age, they become increasingly dependent on the rest of us.

There are more old people around than there used to be for two reasons: firstly, we are better at keeping people alive, so they survive longer, and secondly, efficient birth control has meant that we are better at stopping new ones. The increasing weight of the population at one end of the scale is not being balanced by fresh blood at the other. We have consciously decided to place a high value on the preservation of human life, sometimes regardless of its quality, and consequently we preserve life which goes on to become more expensive to maintain as the years go by. As for their dependence on us and on the health service, it is a result of their deterioration as physical, social and economic beings. Old people need more financial support, more social services, more health care but at the same time as they need more, they contribute less. Their contributions to the community purse were made throughout their working life but they have a shrinking value in an inflationary economy and this is reflected both in their personal savings and pensions, and in the stock of comforts which they have built up. 39% of heads of households over sixty-five live in houses built before 1919 compared with 24% of the rest of us. 20% live in houses without indoor lavatories.[2] The worst conditions of all are reserved for people over eighty, and common sense shows that bad housing, lack of heating, poor diet and social isolation can only intensify the symptoms of illness which might start out simply as a result of age but are aggravated by social problems. As they grow farther away from their working years old people suffer financially. Their pensions don't buy what they used to, and a house which was well-stocked and furnished when they were sixty-five can have deteriorated greatly by the time they reach seventy-five or eighty.

Social dependence is a natural result of an increasingly fragmented society and the breakdown of family life. As society as a whole becomes more affluent, its individual members become increasingly mobile and independent. Children move away from parents to set up home on their own. Young mothers bring up children without the support of grandparents, and the freedom of women to work outside the home means that fewer and fewer of them are in the position to take on the care of an elderly relative. Old people sometimes exaggerate the problem by choosing to spend their last years in communities where they congregate together with other old retired people like themselves, without the benefit of family support and with the hazards that come from putting added strain on the social and medical services in these areas. In at least three coastal towns in England – Worthing, Bexhill and Clacton-on-Sea – the proportion of old people in the community is 25% above the national average. The pressure on geriatric beds in these places is very high, particularly in orthopaedics, because of the tendency of old people to fall more often than the rest of us and to suffer from breaks and sprains. Apart from the distance between old people and their children, who often have no room to take care of an elderly relative, old people may lose their life partners and have nobody of their own age to share life with or to look after them. As a result the inmates of hospitals are more likely than average to be widowed, single or divorced, than married with a competent partner. And more old people stay in hospital because they have no suitable home to be discharged to than because they actually need hospital treatment. 32,000 out of the 36,000 women over seventy-five in non-psychiatric beds are single, widowed or divorced. And as the population grows older still there is the problem of duplicated age where very old parents are in the care of children who are themselves old and may be unable to cope. Apart from which, 25% of the population over sixty-five have no children to care for them at all.

Although old people represent such a visible drain on the health and social services, it is worth remembering that, just like the rest of us, the greater proportion of them continue to live at home. Perhaps 90% of old age pensioners are in the care of their GP and of the local social services rather than the hospital service, although the GP is paid a higher capitation fee for having old age pensioners on his panel as some acknowledgement of the higher demands they make on his time. Moreover, 80% of old people do not live alone, and 86% of old people are visited regularly by their families. None the less, those who do use the health and social services use them very heavily. 50% of all hospital beds – excluding maternity and psychiatry – are occupied by the over sixty-fives, and they use 47% of beds in psychiatric hospitals. Somebody over sixty-five costs the health service £210 a year, as opposed to £85 a year for the rest of us, and that increases the older we get. People over seventy-five cost £240 a year. Some services are much more concentrated on old people than others, and some of these are social rather than medical. Home helps who come in to do general housework spend 87% of their time on the over sixty-fives, and the chiropody service which is so invaluable in keeping people on their feet is almost entirely centred on the old. Money spent in keeping old people in the community like this is money very well spent, both economically, as a preventive measure against the much higher costs of keeping them in hospital, and socially. The greatest problem facing the old is not so much the ravaging effect of a particular acute condition or accident, but the combined effects of sheer boredom and disorientation that result once the control of their own lives is wholly, or in part, removed from them. Nobody disputes that where possible, the goal should be independence and besides, residential accommodation for old people is often very depressing and inadequate.

Old people present peculiar problems to the health services. There is a kind of domino effect that comes into play as we grow old which means that weaknesses and diseases pile up on themselves. By the time we come to die there might be any one of several coexisting conditions that could have been responsible for the death and it is a toss-up which the doctor will choose to write on the death certificate. In a person dying at the age of ninety there are quite likely to be twelve or thirteen separate and possible causes of death. An American study showed that 80% of old people suffer from one or more chronic diseases involving the major organ system such as the heart, the kidney and the brain. Because of this coincidence of ailments they are also likely to be taking several different courses of drugs which can confuse diagnosis – and the patient – still further by their muddle of side-effects. No wonder that the condition most commonly described in old people is 'confusion'. The natural decline of body and mind is hastened in many cases by medical treatment, and is accelerated still further by the decline that takes place once they are taken out of familiar surroundings, and put into care, however kind, however well-meaning, of an institution. Old people, no less than the rest of us, find dependence humiliating. This is particularly so when they know that they suffer from ailments which are socially unacceptable. A great many people, as they grow older, suffer from incontinence. Sometimes incontinence is brought on by the treatment they receive in hospital. A report on nursing care in a hospital ward pointed out how easily this could happen.

Women in their late seventies, eighties and nineties, generally get up during the night to empty their bladders at least once, and often two, three or more times. When admitted to a hospital ward with only one nurse at night in charge of thirty or more patients, there is no chance of the elderly disabled patients being assisted out of bed during the night for this purpose. Inevitably they must allow their bladders to empty in the bed and become incontinent. This not only creates work for the nurse and expense for the hospital, but is quite inhuman and demoralizing for the patient.[3]

What is even more inhuman and demoralizing under these

circumstances is to be blamed or punished like a naughty child. Barbara Robb's horrifying attack on old people's homes and hospital wards, *Sans Everything*, suggested in 1967 that more could be done to reform geriatric nursing by a proper teaching of the physical and psychological reasons for incontinence than anything else.[4] She suggested that kindness was the great need in geriatric care, and recognition of an old patient as an individual with rights to privacy, independence, personal possessions. Her inquiry, along with others conducted into old people's homes and geriatric institutions in the past, has shown conclusively that old people who come into these places are treated like this as part of a rigid regimentation introduced into the pattern of life, and the confusion they feel at being in a strange place among strange people is only intensified.

Looking in from the outside, like any visitor to a geriatric ward or an old people's home, we say, while we still have the strength, will and independence to say it, that nothing could be worse than mouldering away in such a place. When the time comes for us to be looked after, for the reins of our life to be taken from us, we are often past making the choice for ourselves. A second childhood is imposed upon us for everyone else's convenience. A controversial television documentary which showed police film of a mother and daughter apparently colluding in the mother's voluntary euthanasia was almost less shocking for the pressure being put on the mother by the daughter, than for the insensitivity of the kind and caring nuns who descended on the mother later and took away her lethal dose of Nembutal. They talked to an obviously lucid and strong-minded woman as if she were no better than a tiresome toddler, and as if they, not she, were the only people competent to make decisions about her life and the living or the leaving of it. This is a sin of which we are all guilty in talking to the old. If their friends and relatives insist on speaking to, or about, an old person as if he or she were infirm or imbecile, then most old people will respond by reacting to these low expectations. By treating old people in this way we diminish their own capacity to cope with life, to go out alone, to work and travel and take decisions. We make dependants out of them to our own loss. Old people who are capable of leading independent lives in the everyday world can be a source of marvellous inspiration, stimulation and entertainment to people lucky enough to come into contact with them. Is there any medical or social reason why their lives in institutional care should be more limiting than the average nursery? Not every eighty-year-old can be a Bertrand Russell or a Bernard Shaw, and a boring person doesn't get any less boring as he or she grows older, but they don't have to be vegetables either. People at every age put back what is given to them. If people in hospital refer to the old people who seek their help as 'crumblies' – and they do – then something that looks and behaves like a 'crumbly' is what we are all going to end up with.

The attitudes which make crumblies of us all are laid down in society, but they are reflected in the care which old people can expect from the health service. The level of neglect is well illustrated by one health district in the south-east of England, by no means the most ill-served corner of the country, which was visited by the Hospital Advisory Service of the Department of Health and Social Security, a special unit within the National Health Service which has the task of visiting and reporting on conditions in the old long-stay institutions. Reports of the Hospital Advisory Service make fascinating, if gothic reading, and they are a dispassionate and detailed record of some of the worst of what the health service has to offer.

'The Hospital Advisory Service came here,' said the district physician 'and it looked at our services for the elderly and it came up with a *very* critical report. I thought we'd get the black or red edging which means it lands straight on the Minister's desk and you might even get some extra resources, but we didn't even qualify. We were surprised because, basically, we have inadequate everything.'

It is very difficult for those responsible for squeezing capital funds out of the health service to get money for old people. Mostly it is a question of make do and mend, of adapting existing buildings and squeezing into corners that no one else wants. In 1967, *Sans Everything* claimed that mental hospitals – which hold an estimated 60,000 elderly patients – were used simply as dumping grounds for the old and confused people that nobody else would have, and that 80% of elderly patients who suffer with mental problems, have them as a result of un-treated physical symptoms. One of the root causes of the second-class treatment of many old people within the health service is the attitude of the medical profession to the elderly. If old people are dumped in mental institutions and in local authority homes and long-stay wards, it is often because the GP and community services which he authorizes, are no longer pre-pared or able to take responsibility for their care, or because he sees the intolerable pressure which the care of a dependent old person can put on an otherwise self-sufficient family. Old people are certainly not very welcome in the teaching hospitals either. Despite the very high proportion of them in the average district hospital, they are not considered the right kind of in-spirational teaching material for impressionable young medical students, and one professor in a well-known teaching hospital was reported in a Hospital Advisory Service report as saying that his students should not be contaminated by contact with geriatric patients. It is doubtful if this professor, or any teacher in a British medical school adopts the imaginative technique of an American geriatrician who handicaps his students with ear-plugs, distorting eye-glasses and numbness in order to give them an insight into the isolation of old age.

There is a body of medical opinion which thinks that ger-iatrics has no business being a separate speciality in the first place. Old people, they say, are just people grown old, nothing special or different from the rest of us. But if this is true, and this is what doctors really think, then why are old people treated so differently? The Department of Health and Social Security recommends that the existence of a properly defined geriatric service could ease the pressures on hospital services by increas-ing the turnover of patients, by reducing waiting lists, by step-ping in before irreversible deterioration has taken place and by taking the pressure off general hospital beds. They argue for the placing of geriatric wards within the body of a normal district hospital as a means of reducing the isolation of geriatricians and improving contact within the medical profession. Certainly a policy of integration would improve the contact of old people with the community, and do something to reduce the ill-effects of isolation in old wards and homes, the boredom and apathy that muffle the path to death.

Treatment of geriatrics as a speciality also means that the people who work with the old could develop a special understanding of the problems that come with physical decline. Age can distort the norms found in medical text-books, and symptoms can often express themselves differently in an old body from a young one. Sensitivity to pain decreases with age, and the signs of disease can present themselves in more vague and disguised forms than they would in a younger patient. And, as we have seen, drugs can have a confusing effect on old people which leads to a high rate – 15% – of iatrogenic (or doctor-caused) illness. One experiment in this field proved that by taking a group of elderly patients off barbiturates they became much more mentally normal and lucid. In fact, more like real people.

It seems likely that any future planning for old people will be much more concerned with their treatment as real people, with the need to guard their independence and self-control as long as possible. The lack of facilities in the community and, above all, the very confusing tangle of different services available for old people, often leads to their hospitalization, but this is proving too expensive for us, both in financial and social terms. There is growing emphasis on the provision of day care for old people but the funds aren't there. The current effort at providing more care for the elderly seems to be concentrating on the switch of under-used resources from other branches of the health service, such as maternity, with consequent uproar and protest among the general population who respond more warmly to the thought of little babies than they do to the limited appeal of the old. Voluntary help is far more crucial in this field than in any other, and it is fortunate for the strained resources of the health ser-

C

vice and the social services that so many people are happy to give up time and money to old people, even to those unrelated to them. Public indifference is leavened by a strong and active streak of caring and social responsibility.

Although the situation has improved in the last ten years, you would be very hard put to it to find anyone who has ever worked with old people in an institution who would willingly put their relatives under the same kind of treatment. The old and the chronically infirm are the patients who suffer most from the biases that are built into our idea of what a health service is. What lies at the root of our treatment of the old is a rejection of the *memento mori*, a closure of the mind to the inescapable fact that old people are us. As a contributor to *Sans Everything* writes:

By consigning the elderly with such thoughtlessness, and often with such deception to those vast and crowded pools of helplessness which we are content to accept as their last refuge, we brand ourselves as a society which, far from honouring old people, tries to banish old age completely from the mind.

With an extraordinary and dogged capacity for self-deception we refuse to admit to ourselves the fact that the way we treat our parents and grandparents is the way in which we ourselves may expect to be treated. When an adult shows disrespect or contempt towards an elderly person in the sight and hearing of someone even younger, he is imprinting the same attitude on to the next generation. It should cause him no astonishment, bewilderment or alarm when the time comes to be dependent on his children, if those same children, well taught and conditioned, fling him on to the same old scrap-heap without ceremony or care. If we meet a geriatrician at a party and fail to be as impressed as we would have been had we met a famous heart surgon, then we can hardly be surprised if that same geriatrician fails to squeeze the resources he needs to give adequate care and attention to his patients, out of the health service, or out of the community, which bestows its smiles, its attention and its cash on something more instantly rewarding. Doctors receive their kudos from the value which their colleagues – and the public – put on their work. Old people are rather short of kudos.

'Go round any hospital you like,' says a doctor 'and see for yourself the large number of elderly people in it. 60 to 70% of our bed days are taken up with the elderly. Two thirds of the hospital budget goes on the elderly. So given these facts – and what you see with your own eyes – you think, "That's funny. That's not talked about very much." But the reason is that caring for the elderly carries a very low status. Just think of the trouble old people cause when they go mad or become incontinent or helpless. The status, the acceptability of caring for the elderly is very low.'

In 1959 the Department of Health issued a circular on the need to improve services for old people. In 1971 it issued another circular on the same theme. In 1976, and again in 1977, it stated its firm intention to give priority to services for old people. In other words, its good intentions have lasted some twenty years without any noticeable change in the service. The reasons at the bottom of the whole problem go much deeper than the logistical difficulties of shifting resources within a government-run service. Until we all show as much interest in the caring role of the health service as we do in its emergency work, and until all of us, doctors, health workers and the general public, learn to connect these dependent people at the end of life with our vigorous, independent and self-centred selves, another twenty years may pass with no visible change.

II. Out of Sight, Out of Mind

The problems of mental health, like those of old age, are something that affect all of us but which we prefer to ignore. We throw the mentally ill and handicapped, like the old, on to the shoulders of the health service to be carried away and dealt with as far from the rest of us as possible. We would rather not be contaminated with the infection of abnormality which frightens us all the more because it lurks beneath the surface of all our lives. The patients of the mental health service are people like us, but not quite the same as us, reminders of what we could become and what we might be, half-nightmares that we prefer to keep in the back of our collective mind. The days of humouring the village idiot, or of visiting Bedlam for a sociable laugh at the loonies are over. Today we really prefer not to know.

And yet the problems of mental health touch us all more closely than ever. Five million of us present ourselves to our GPs each year with a mental health problem. Mental illness loses Britain twenty-four million working days a year. These figures refer to cases where mental stress and illness are the open and acknowledged cause of the problem. They don't take into account the much larger, uncounted number of cases that have a component of mental illness in them which hasn't risen so obviously to the surface. Who knows how many physical symptoms are tied to mental distress, or how they should be treated? Of the five million, over half a million of us go on to be referred to the specialized psychiatric services and may end up as in-patients in a psychiatric hospital. Our chances of spending part of our lives in a psychiatric ward are very high. One in six for women, and one in nine for men. Nobody could call mental health a minor problem.

45% of all hospital beds are occupied by the mentally ill and handicapped but it is an indication of the neglect into which the services have fallen – or from which they have never risen – that only 25% of the hospital budget is spent in their care. The cost per in-patient week for the mentally handicapped in 1974–5 was £33·68 and for the mentally ill it was £36·60. For a patient in a London teaching hospital the cost was £154·22. However, we spent over £46 million on drugs which affect the mind, on tranquillizers, anti-depressants and hypnotics. If the drugs which the GP prescribes fail – and he hardly has the time to pull up the roots of every patient's mental health problem and examine them closely – the patient may well find himself referred to some of the worst facilities in the health service in terms of provision of staff, buildings and money. As with the old people, a golden future lies in the better provision of community care, in helping people to overcome their illness in the surroundings with which they will have to cope later, and with the support of family and friends. But in the meantime, a large proportion of the hospitals for the mentally ill and handicapped are great Victorian ships that pass in the night, cruising along with their full loads of passengers off the mainland of society. In Scotland, 90% of hospitals in the psychiatric service were built in the nineteenth century. Throughout the British Isles patients inhabit buildings which were designed for different times as the concrete representation of old ideas. The huge mental illness hospitals of the nineteenth century were designed for the two-way protection of patient and public, to be self-sufficient, isolated communities, many of them to have 2,000 patients and more. London is still surrounded with a ring of such hospitals, placed out in the Home Counties to cope with London patients well away from the city centre, far from the communities from which the patients originally came.

The worst of them are vivid concrete representations of what it must mean to be mad. From a distance they are sinister enough, isolated in their leafy parks and grounds. Inside they are often no more reassuring, despite the brave efforts that may have been made to cheer them up with bright paint or flowers or personal possessions. They have great long corridors like lessons in perspective, overcrowded wards where beds and lockers huddle impersonally together beneath high ceilings and every vestige of personality has been erased to be replaced with the institutional variety of different-coloured candlewick bedspreads. Among the patients there is all the apathy and hopelessness associated with a high population of lifeless old people. Their vast numbers and their desolation have tended to freeze psychiatric services into an inescapable pattern. Even outside Britain, in America and in the countries of the EEC the situation is the same. The average size of a psychiatric hospital is 1,200 beds and in the worst hospitals the patients can be concentrated into wards which hold up to 50 patients.[5]

'In the days when there were 1,820 patients in this hospital,' said one psychiatrist, 'they had to climb over each other's beds to get in and out. It was the Dark Ages. Sanitary towels were being sent to the laundry and washed for re-use. When the matron arrived here in 1955, 300 otherwise healthy women were being kept in bed all the time because it was easier for the staff.'

Even experienced health professionals can return from visits to places like this deeply depressed and disturbed by the way of life that continues within their walls. The very low cost of keeping a patient in a psychiatric hospital is some indication of the quality of life. The cost of medical staff in mental health is 26% that of acute medicine. The staff, medical, nursing and even support staff will be largely foreign. The services that go to maintain day-to-day life will be inferior. Even the food bills are lower than they would be in the average general hospital. Everything indicates that a mental health problem brings with it a lowering of the quality of life on every front, and that these generally observed aspects of life in mental health institutions – the poor surroundings, the lack of highly qualified medical staff, the high proportion of immigrant staff – are common to most countries in the world. By being sick or dependent enough to enter the world of a psychiatric hospital, a patient relinquishes a little of his right to be treated as a human being.

Long-term aims for the mental health service include a much higher concentration on prevention, on the desegregation of the mentally ill and handicapped, on keeping people out of institutions as much and as long as possible and treating them as out patients, on providing community support and follow-up. In mental health, as in all the other backward areas of the health service, liaison with the social services is the key, but it seems to be a very stiff key that resists turning. How can people be treated as out patients and have easy access to help when adequate facilities don't exist universally in local hospitals, and when the specialized units are so generally far from the towns? A bravely optimistic note in the government *Priorities* document mentions no hospitals larger than 200 beds, but in England and Wales there are 24 hospitals of over 1,500 beds, and figures hovering just under 1,000 patients are far from rare.

A further need, perhaps one of the most frighteningly urgent in the mental health services, is for facilities to treat those patients who are positively dangerous and need to be kept under conditions of high security. The main security units in England – Broadmoor, Rampton, Moss Side and Park Lane – are dangerously overcrowded, but the problem of moving their patients out into the care of other hospitals is an acute one, even where conditions of high security may no longer be necessary for them. Nobody wants to be involved in the risks of treating patients who are likely to be violent, inhumanly strong when roused and utterly unpredictable, particularly not the nursing staff who are in the most constant contact with their patients and all the problems which they pose. The strength of the nursing unions within mental health hospitals has given them greater powers of resistance to the patients they don't want. Although the government has made special allocations of money to each region to make provision for these patients and has the official policy of establishing a high-security unit in each region, this has proved to be mere pie in the sky. The money has mostly vanished on other priorities outside psychiatric medicine and as for the provision of high security units, the ways of prevaricating and blocking plans and decisions appear to be limitless when it comes to having dangerous patients parked on your own doorstep.

As with almost every other form of illness that costs society a great deal to treat, the imaginative use of prevention could solve a great many mental health problems before they became intractable, but in mental illness the social factors are so paramount that it would require a wholesale transformation of modern industrial society into a utopia before everyday life could be said to be entirely conducive to health and happiness. Too many aspects of twentieth-century life militate against peace of mind. People who have very high-tension, demanding jobs, which afflict them with ulcers, insomnia and all the symptoms of stress, are candidates for mental breakdown. So are people who have to do extremely repetitive, boring, undemanding jobs and who live in unsatisfactory, overcrowded conditions, or work in the ceaseless din and inhumanity of the modern factory. So is someone who is unemployed. A woman struggling to look after small children in the isolation of a slum room or a high-rise flat, is an obvious candidate for anxiety and depression. So is the single career girl with no family support. People who live in sub-standard conditions, people who live alone, people who suffer from sexual problems, people with no sexual outlet, people who are pressured into feeling inadequate, or who are pressured to achieve success beyond their capacity, are all potential victims of mental illness. The lack of community support and of a spiritual basis to modern life is of no help in providing calm or stability, so that the role of the priest, the comforter and the trusted confessor falls upon the doctor.

In mental handicap, a field where most of the problems are congenital, preventive measures could much more easily be taken if only the interest and the cash could be provided. Already there are reliable and available tests for the detection of certain conditions such as mongolism, which, allied with ease of abortion and counselling for the parents, could prevent the birth of handicapped individuals who are likely to place great strain on the family and the community. Better ante-natal care and health education have been proved to play a vital part in the birth of healthy, intelligent children.

However, most of us are born healthy and in possession of our faculties. What happens to make us lose our control of life, to alienate us from the people round us, reduce our ability to cope with the simplest decisions, fragment us from reality? What are those five million people a year suffering from? Even five million may be an under estimate. One off-the-cuff figure from a psychiatrist says that 25% of the population suffer from some kind of mental disturbance, and in certain places – midtown Manhattan, for example – it may be as high as four out of five. A psychiatric unit will see people suffering from depression, from phobic states – unreasonable fear of anything from confined places to spiders – anxiety, sexual problems. A quarter of the patients who present themselves to one of the biggest mental hospitals turn out to be suffering from what the staff call the Big Four – impotence, frigidity, vaginismus and premature ejaculation. Mental illness is something that historically brings shame and stigma with it. We are afraid to report symptoms because we think we will look weak or foolish, or we are afraid of being thought mad and put away. But mental illness is no respecter of persons. It is something that can affect anyone at any age and in many forms. One-third of referrals from the GP to the psychiatric service are what are classed as neurotics, people who retain their consciousness of the real world but whose capacity to cope with it is diminished, people suffering from anxiety, depression or high tension. At an estimate, 20 men and 47 women in 1,000 suffer from anxiety neurosis. One person in 300 is a schizophrenic, a member of a group which suffers from psychotic conditions where the patient loses touch with reality. And the third large class of psychiatric disorders is psychopathic; people with no moral sense, no feeling of guilt or responsibility, often coupled with extremely aggressive or violent conduct. The difficulty which we have in understanding what different mental illnesses actually mean comes in part from the frequency and carelessness with which psychiatric terms have entered every day language and life. It is very common to hear somebody referred to as a psychopath, a neurotic or a schizo, without the person using the term meaning it as much more than a generalized insult.

More people suffer from these various conditions than the service can happily cope with. 835 full-time psychiatric consultants share the responsibility for a quarter of a million adult in-patients each year, added to one and a half million out-patients and two million day patients. Even allowing for overlap, it is easy to see that the sheer volume of patients means that very few of them will get to see a consultant psychiatrist in the course of their illness. Under this pressure of patients to be seen, and given the limitations of the service in terms of poor physical surroundings, and equally high pressure on junior medical and nursing staff, what can the service do to alleviate the country's mental health problems? What it obviously can't do is to reach out any further than its own gates and tackle the mass of people with a potential mental health problem, or do anything to prevent the growing crop of patients from needing emergency help.

'What this hospital does very well,' said one psychiatrist, 'is to run emergency services for acute mental illness. We can take people in straight from home or via the police or the social services. What we aren't good at providing is psychological treatment for distressed people who haven't actually broken down.'

What they can't do either, without an enormous increase in help from the community at large and from the social service departments, is put back into the community those patients who no longer need the acute treatment of a mental hospital. There are fewer patients in hospitals than there used to be but as a hospital pointed out drily, 'the current decline in patients is accounted for not by rehabilitation but by death'. 95% of patients in psychiatric hospitals are theoretically free to discharge themselves, but lack of support and follow-up in the outside world keeps them in the comparative shelter of the wards. It may surprise some people to know that despite the depressing population of the old and senile in psychiatric hospitals, the average length of stay is under one month. Even in cases of mental handicap, over half the patients are in hospitals for stays of less than three months, probably accounted for by patients passing through for assessment, but the next highest percentage, nearly 20%, are in hospital for five years or more.

If you can imagine anything so lowly, mental handicap is the ugly sister of mental illness. A mental handicap hospital, particularly one which houses children, can be an acutely depressing and disturbing place for someone who is not used to seeing such concentrated evidence of human damage and disability. We can all become mentally ill, but mental handicap is usually something with which you are born. If mental illness is a backwater, then mental handicap is an oxbow lake. There is an attitude in society which is reflected, if not always overtly voiced in the medical profession, that the answer to mental handicap is euthanasia and not the investment of time, patience and hard work that goes into mentally handicapped patients if they are lucky. People who work in mental handicap and who retain any sense of optimism and interest in their patients are revolted by this attitude. More than half the patients in any given institution for the mentally handicapped might be perfectly capable of rehabilitation and discharge into the community, given the proper aftercare. There is a large legacy of patients admitted in the days when to be not too bright, and in need of care and protection, was enough to get you admitted to an institution. Often these patients are no more stupid than a great number of people outside the institution who carry out quite normal lives, but the over-protection of the hospital has done more harm than good, and institutional life has robbed otherwise normal people of the ability to make the small decisions that leading an independent life involves.

More severely handicapped people – those suffering from severe epilepsy, spastics, mongols, children brain-damaged at birth, people who will never be capable of leading independent lives – need the full-time care and attention that health professionals can give, but other problems which look intractable to laymen are proving responsive to treatment by dedicated staff. Behaviour problems can be ironed out by constant and concentrated effort on the part of staff, and the families of mentally handicapped children can be given the moral and emotional support that enables them to carry on. It is the stigma attached to mental handicap – the deeply rooted belief that mentally handicapped children are incapable of learning or improvement, that mentally handicapped adults would be a danger at large in the community, that nothing in mental handicap responds to the magic of modern medicine – that holds back the services and starves them of funds and the support that could transform them from a depressing and largely custodial service to one which cares, and even positively cures.

Because of the inextricable mixture of social and physical elements – the unscientific and unproven aspect of much of the treatment of mental ill health, the sheer squalor of the surroundings in which much of it is undertaken – the psychiatrist, and still more the doctor in mental handicap, must struggle hard for their status in the medical profession. With its heavy concentration on the mechanistic, purely physical side of medicine, the mind and all its problems get very little space, if any, in the average medical school curriculum. Psychiatrists tend to get drawn into their career once they have finished their initial training, sometimes because, given the comparative lack of competition in psychiatry, their chances of winning a consultancy are much higher than they would be in general medicine or obstetrics. The existence of a Royal College of Psychiatrists is doing what it can to up the prestige and influence of its members, but it still has a long way to go. The rewards of psychiatry are low. 'Other Royal Colleges get left large sums of money by grateful patients,' said a member of the Royal College of Psychiatrists, 'but in psychiatry you don't get grateful patients.'

'How do you get your job satisfaction?' asks a consultant in mental handicap. 'If you get it from giving someone a drug and then three weeks later they're better, this is not for you. Instant success is not in it. With appendicitis, ten days later the patient is cured. In mental subnormality you see the patient for the rest of his life.'

With the results so undramatic and care so long-term, the role of the mental health services has grown up uneasily divided between the purely custodial and the curative. The punitive element in treating mental illness which has always been there has been somewhat reduced, but there is still an element of social ostracism to being a patient in a mental institution. Even though the 1959 Mental Health Act emphasized the hospital's role as a place of treatment rather than simply a place of custody, a dumping ground for the difficult and unlovable, the curative value of much treatment is both suspect and wide open to dispute. With the impossible uneven ratio of medical staff to patients, choice of treatment is limited. Some techniques, like psychoanalysis, which are well known by reputation to the layman, are utterly impractical in a psychiatric hospital because they require the one element that is almost completely absent, and that is lots and lots of time. Psychiatric opinion is split in two basic directions on treatment of the patients admitted to them. One school prefers treatment by the growing number of psychotropic drugs. The other inclines towards therapy by talking, by social activity, by human contact and human care. Some combine the two systems. Modern treatment is certainly more demanding of staff time than it used to be, though the use of drugs has helped enormously in calming patients so that they become more tractable and less demanding. In the past the weight of patients to available nursing staff meant that a great many patients did nothing at all. It was simpler for everybody if they were simply kept in their beds or chairs all day, or maybe outside in the cages, and netted in to their beds at night. Any kind of active treatment disturbed the even tenor of the nurse's ways. The change of function from custodial to curative means a great change in nursing attitudes, as well as education.

'More is asked of us,' said one, 'because in the past it was easier to allow the patients to do nothing, to sit and stare at each other and talk back to their voices.'

In mental handicap, in particular, the tendency in progressive units is for patients to be much more heavily involved in some kind of activity and positive treatment. In one good hospital they make sure that only 15 people out of 490 patients are not involved in some kind of activity whether it is behaviour modification, industrial light work or simply dancing and music. The national average of patient occupation is nearer 50%. Of course the techniques of behaviour modification and patient work applied at this hospital are very demanding of staff time, and the days when the nurses could clear the ward in the morning and spend the rest of the day undisturbed in their own routine are gone. Behaviour modification requires a one-to-one relationship between staff and patient to teach, by constant repetition, reward and correction, the most basic social aptitudes like toilet training, or how not to bang your head against a brick wall. The greatest difference to the course of a mental illness or to the development of a mentally handicapped child could be made by catching the patient in time, but the resources of the service are so restricted that they invariably come too late and are only brought in to deal with the worst, the most advanced cases.

'If we can get children at an early age,' says the teacher in mental handicap, 'we can correct faults. We can teach and help parents with a handicapped child how to cope. Left alone with a mentally subnormal or disturbed child the parents withdraw. They feel unique. Then they come here, they talk to other parents and they find out that they're not unique. What happens otherwise is that they get over-protective. If you do that with a subnormal child he'll start manipulating the parents and become a damned nuisance. We have children who at the age of twelve of fourteen can't dress themselves because the mother hadn't made them do it as infants. Some children become very disturbed. Many have behaviour problems because of a *laissez faire* attitude when they were small. Pinching bottoms is O.K. when you're a little kid but it's not funny at fourteen. Time is the most important factor. Parents feel that a subnormal child can't learn anything – lots of people think this, even in the medical profession. You'll get doctors in other specialities who'll refuse to operate on a mentally handicapped child. They'll think, "It's a spastic, why should I bother?" But two handicaps are worse than one.'

Late admission means that the problem is already much more difficult, but in both mental handicap and mental illness there is often no room to admit any but the patient whose condition is obviously advanced enough to need treatment. A patient is admitted to a psychiatric hospital when he needs continual nursing or medical care, when supervision is necessary or when it is simply impossible for him to remain at home, sometimes because home circumstances are at the root of the disturbance in the first place. Occasionally there is a clear-cut need for the people around him, or even complete strangers, to be protected from his behaviour.

'So what role should the hospital have?' asks a psychiatrist. 'Should we be a dustbin for all society's failures? It is more difficult to make a clear-cut decision in a psychiatric hospital. In a general hospital you can't turn down an acute abdomen for admission, it's something which clearly needs medical treatment. But if you've got someone who's pissed and starts wrecking the house, is it mental illness? Or is it wickedness to be pursued in the courts? We have someone today – a retired major, panicky, hypochondriacal, anxious, suicidal. He wants to come into the hospital. Out patients have done him no good. Now straightforward mental illness like this is obviously what we're primarily here for. Then other problems arise once they're in. Go to our recreation ward and you'll see that we've got TV, billiards, tropical fish, plenty of female patients to chat to – people can be institutionalized in here overnight.'

The problems that are caused by inadequate investment in mental health services are largely social ones. Where a patient is admitted too late, the family, the job, the marriage may already have suffered beyond repair. There is no advice given, no helping hand stretched out until it is too late. In the past it was almost too easy to be admitted. Mental hospitals were used as rubbish tips for social casualties, for people unwanted by their families, for girls who got pregnant, for consistently antisocial behaviour. Nowadays the criteria for admission are much stiffer. Behaviour has to be extremely antisocial and difficult for a patient to need admission, like the girl who consistently takes all her clothes off in public. Is she simply seeking attention? Is it her way of making sexual advances? Concentrated care found that she only ever did it when men were around, and by consistent attention and correction she was eventually cured of the habit and considered suitable for return to the community. Some of the patients, of course, don't want to come out into the community any more than we want them there. They need the protection of a sheltered environment. But for the rest of them, good mental health services could give the caring and build up the confidence that is necessary.

There has been a great effort in recent years to return to the community all those patients who could reasonably be considered capable of looking after themselves without needing constant medical or nursing attention, and without behaviour problems so severe that they might be considered an embarrassment or a danger to the community. But a kind of natural limit seems to have been reached. By admitting only at the last minute, the patients who do get into hospital are in a much worse condition, and by moving out those who are eligible, the patients who are most dependent, in particular the old and senile, remain. The great advances in drug therapy have allowed doctors to control patients more easily and diminished the need for locked wards, but the most difficult patients can resist even the power of drugs, and it is on the nursing staff that the burden of their care, and even the physical danger they represent, falls most heavily. Intermittent scandals, occasional reports on cruelty to patients, or on violence inside psychiatric hospitals, highlight the abnormality of a nurse's life inside the mental health services. It is no wonder that studies into conditions hint that the psychiatric nursing staff is not always like its counterpart in acute hospitals. 'Psychiatric hospitals,' said one report, 'tend to attract a higher proportion of apathetic, ignorant or frankly mentally ill doctors and nurses than others. There are hospitals where the sick are in the hands of the very sick indeed. After six months in certain hospitals there are ways in which psychiatric nurses are no longer like other people. They become numbed to old age, cruelty, the dying.'[6]

That was written ten years ago and times have certainly moved on. There have been determined and successful attempts to improve the standards of staffing both among nursing and medical staff. It would be grossly unfair to the many dedicated and younger staff to suggest that the picture now was as black as that, but nobody who was concerned for the mental health services would deny that there is still a long way to go. Psychiatric nurses are different in many ways from nurses in general hospitals. They are more likely to be men, partly because the job often demands sheer physical strength to deal with unruly patients. They are still suffering from the gradual change of role that has overtaken them as the service has tried to leave behind its more custodial duties in favour of positive caring and treatment. The older school of psychiatric nurses may have come into the service for reasons that were not purely humanitarian.

'A lot of people came into psychiatric nursing during the slump,' explained a psychiatrist. 'A lot were colliers and they brought with them a tradition of trade unionism. The unions have always been strong in mental hospitals. This shows itself in the preferential salary scales, in optional retirement at fifty-five. After twenty years in the mental health service each year counts as double towards your pension, and there's more holidays. There's also more absenteeism because it's an ageing population.'

Whatever the background of nurses in mental health, they are increasingly more important to the care and treatment of the patient than the doctor, because the doctors are so few and far between, and those that there are are often – even predominantly – foreign. In psychiatry, more than in any other medical speciality, comprehension between doctor and patient is vitally important. Quite crucial misunderstandings can occur if the doctor and patient fail to understand each other, if language difficulties confuse the consultation, and if different cultural background prevents the significance of a patient's problem from being understood. It is ironic, and it is one of the most basic problems facing the mental health services, that in the one area where verbal and cultural communication between doctor and patient is of paramount importance, the highest proportion of the medical staff are least likely to understand.

In both areas of the mental health service it has been agreed that the future solution lies in improved community care. Isolating patients in awful old buildings, with staff who are not in the best position to sort out their problems is not a satisfactory answer. While a large number of patients, particularly the old, will continue to require some kind of sheltered and supportive environment, a strong back-up service with easily accessible out patient facilities would keep thousands of prospective patients in contact with the rest of us and on the way to leading a normal life. But it seems that we don't really want to know. We are afraid that people who suffer from mental and behaviour problems will embarrass us, behave oddly in the street, lower property values and frighten our children. Social services are unprepared for the new pressures that would be put on them if a semi-dependent population were suddenly to be housed in the community, so they adopt a *laissez-faire* attitude and make sure that the problem stays within the health service.

'Half the population of this hospital could be in the community tomorrow if homes were available,' said a consultant, 'but the social services don't want people discharged because it means more work for them. If you suggest putting handicapped people in a new housing area they'll be accepted, but in established residential areas they're considered nothing but trouble. People feel they can't cope, they'll be noisy, they'll expose themselves, they'll attack people. "They" is the problem, as if a mental patient is peculiar. The stereotyping is the biggest problem. In fact alternative services simply don't exist. There's no ratepayers' money, just a lot of hypocritical statements. There's no voting potential in mental health.'

The patients we want least of all are the violent patients, and it is not just the general public who will resist the building of a high-security unit anywhere within miles of its back garden. They are the unwanted patients inside the service as well. Whatever site is projected for the building of a high-security unit is objected to violently by local residents and politicians, and movement out of a high-security unit into a normal psychiatric hospital capable of dealing with improved patients is equally resisted, partly as a result of the increased power of the psychiatric nurses.

'Should we be expected to take patients from Rampton and Broadmoor just because we have locked facilities?' asked a psychiatrist from one of the hospitals which is fitted to take them. 'The nurses have said they won't nurse patients from secure units. As a result of our clinical freedom, Rampton and Broadmoor are silting up. People are copping out of their responsibilities. We ought to be here offering end-rehabilitation after the person is fit to be discharged from the secure unit, but every so often something goes wrong. This is one of the crises in the psychiatric services that is coming up, the unwillingness of the hospitals to take these cases on transfer because of the power of the nurses. The nurses don't want trouble or danger and there is a crisis of authority.'

Throughout the psychiatric services there is a readiness to rehabilitate patients but we, the public, won't cooperate. If a patient gets stuck in a mental hospital for more than two years then his chances of getting out are greatly reduced, though the population is theoretically less narrow-minded about mental health, more ready to receive patients than it once was. A great deal of coverage and explanation is given on mental illness through the press and television, and every single one of us knows someone on tranquillizers even if we don't take them ourselves. This dissemination of information, this gradual familiarity with the problem offers the best hope of erasing the stigma attached to it and preparing the public to welcome patients from psychiatric hospitals, or people with a mental problem, into the community. Attitudes are changing but not, it seems, fast enough. The mental health services are still struggling impecuniously out of the nineteenth century, and until we ourselves open our minds, pockets and doors to their patients, they may never escape.

5 Stopping the Gaps

The long-stay areas within medicine itself are not the only examples of neglect in the health service. There are two other primary ways in which misuse of medical manpower can affect the quality of a health service, quite apart from its uneven spread between medical specialities. One is in actual geographical distribution of health care, something which often goes hand in hand with inter-speciality distribution and shares some of the problems of cause and effect. The other is in actual use of medical time, in the distribution of work between doctors and other health care workers, particularly nurses, which can lead to relatively simple tasks being done by over-skilled, over-trained and consequently over-paid people. The strongest resistance to the delegation of medical tasks comes from within the medical profession itself, although there is growing evidence that more imaginative use of ancillary workers in the health service can help to solve a great many of the problems of which doctors complain.

It is very hard for the average member of the public, with a vague interest in the health service and its problems, to gather whether we actually have too few doctors or too many. We are undeniably short of doctors in certain areas, and yet there is an underlying panic that we may be in the process of training too many for the work available. In fact the basic question of whether a country has too many or too few doctors cannot be answered without considering the vital information which tells us what they actually do. In Britain, the ratio of doctors to patients is approximately 1·25 per 1,000 people. This compares and ·001 per 1,000 in Ethiopia. Doctors, like the administrators with 1·6 per 1,000 in the United States, 2·4 per 1,000 in Russia they resent, have a facility for reproducing themselves. Between 1949 and 1970 the number of doctors in Britain went up by

131% although the population as a whole went up by only 6%, and when doctors grow in number, so do the support staff working alongside them. In a survey of Western medicine conducted by McKinsey and Co., the number of people employed in any health service per 10,000 population worked out between the different survey countries at about 150 individuals – about 15 doctors, 2 nurses, 4 dentists, 5 pharmacists and 100 miscellaneous supporting staff.[1] On average 4% of the working population is employed in the health business, although no other country houses such a proportionately large employer as the British Health Service.

However, the excellence of a country's health service cannot be judged by sheer volume of manpower. Everything depends on how that manpower is used. Despite the slightly lower proportion of doctors to patients in Britain than in the United States, their skills are nevertheless more efficiently used because of their wider distribution, and because of the existence of an efficient primary care system, the general practitioner service – which rations and balances the use of more expensive specialist skills. In America a survey showed that 60% of the doctors questioned gave some primary care whatever their discipline.[2] They included cardiologists, rheumatologists, dermatologists and especially psychiatrists who, in America according to the report 'have usurped the functions of the family confessor, who alone among doctors still has the time to talk to his patients and who attends to thousands of women and men who would be at a loss if asked to name their family doctor'. Patients who use specialist doctors in this way are abusing expensive skills and undergoing a potentially extravagant process of self-diagnosis – extravagant because, if they are wrong, they have to pay the first bill before moving on. The existence of the general practitioner as the easily understood and approachable point of access to the whole health and social services network makes for a much better use of the service. General practitioners in Britain deal with 90% of the illness in the population without any further reference to other health services, and they account for only 20% of the health service budget. From a health service point of view a G P system is a very good buy. A bad G P, from the health service point of view, if not the patient's, is one who refers unnecessarily without taking the responsibility of treatment upon himself, thus clogging up out patient departments and laboratories with minor problems and complaints.

But even within the G P service there are areas of bad and inadequate service, and within the hospital services these failures are equally visible. Once again the clinical freedom, which is essential to the doctor's relationship with his individual patient, acts as a stumbling block to the establishment of a rational health service. The free choice exercised by doctors over the way they work, what they do, where they do it and for whom, creates an imbalance in the distribution of services that is even more noticeable in countries where free enterprise operates, than it is in countries with some degree of central control. At times this unbounded freedom can even be seen to operate directly against the doctors' interests. In some Latin-American countries where no bar is exercised over entry to the medical profession, the consequent abundant supply of medical graduates find themselves barely scratching a living. In cities like Cordoba in Argentina, the ratio of doctors to patients is 1:170, and some doctors consequently find themselves earning no more than the average labourer.[3]

The problems of maldistribution of medical care which the developed countries face are to be seen in their most extreme form in the countries of the Third World where the problems are aggravated by the implantation of Western standards and practices on to teeming, poor, rural communities, which can't possibly afford to implement them. The increasing imbalance in the treatment of urban and rural communities is often only exaggerated by the training of health personnel, especially doctors, in sophisticated and costly Western practices and habits which the country can't afford to indulge, and which render the doctors themselves unfit for considering the real needs of the people they have to treat. In Ethiopia, to take one example, Western aid built a very large and sophisticated hospital in the centre of Addis Ababa to train Ethiopian doctors. Operated at full capacity, the hospital is capable of swallowing up 45% of the country's entire health budget.[4] Outside the capital the proportion of doctors to population is 1:65,000, and 90% of the rural population live at least a day's walk from even a feeder track. The doctors trained in such a hospital are not on the whole interested in moving to such isolated conditions. In India, the proportion of doctors to people is 1:400 in the great urban communities of Calcutta or Bombay, but out in the countryside it is 1 to between 30 and 45,000.[5] The fact that doctors are trained largely in a hospital setting to practise acute curative medicine, is no preparation for the quite different approach needed in rural areas, nor does the way in which all doctors are trained prepare them mentally for the way of life of a rural doctor. Two young Indians who were sent into the countryside after the normal urban hospital training found themselves so alienated from the way of life, the people and the work that they committed suicide.

The situation in essence, though not in degree, is similar in the richer countries of the West. In the United States where the most sophisticated medicine available is practised on one quarter of the population while large areas of the country go undoctored, the biggest differential is race. Black women are three times as likely to die of complications in pregnancy as white women because they receive less antenatal care.[6] Even among the white population the infant mortality rate in the best state is half that of the worst. Distribution among medical specialties is as unequal as it is between regions, and even between areas and classes in the same city. The attractions of high incomes to be earned on the fee-for-service system lures doctors into surgery with the result that the rate of surgery is twice as high in America as in Britain, although, almost certainly, not twice as necessary. Nor is there any reason for the British to feel smug at the sight of inequalities suffered by countries with a less socially just health system than the NHS. Despite thirty years of the Welfare State, a baby born in a well-equipped teaching hospital is between three and four times as likely to survive the first week of life as a baby born in certain parts of rural England or in the North. An unskilled labourer between the ages of fifteen and sixty-four is twice as likely to die of the commonest diseases as a member of social class one, almost three times as likely to die of cancer of the lung and nearly seven times as likely to die of bronchitis. He is even more likely to die of coronary heart disease, despite that condition's common association with affluence and good living. The overall death rate for the same group is twice as high as for social class one and the same sharp contrast in death-rates shows itself between different regions. Mortality in South Wales, for example, is 28% higher than in East Anglia. Evidently the quality of the health service is far from being the only factor involved, but the distribution and quality of health services seems to be doing little to redress the balance.

Every health service in the world faces the problem of persuading the medical profession to go where it is most needed. The Royal Commission on Medical Education commented:

we have found from our own inquiries that no country in the world has really succeeded in persuading recent medical graduates to serve in outlying areas, where they are necessarily denied access to specialized medical facilities and the constant company of other doctors, with its important implications for maintaining professional competence and the amenities of social life which a highly educated young person normally expects.

Only Norway, of all the Western countries, has had any noticeable success in filling posts in remote rural areas, and one would imagine that the magical ingredient found by the Norwegian government was not simply higher payment, but the opportunity for the doctor to move on after a fixed period of service.

The unplanned, almost unpremeditated response of most health services to this universal problem of maldistribution is the use of immigrant labour. Where the tide of medical skill washes itself so unevenly over the population, the gaps are filled for us by a regular influx of immigrant doctors. The situ-

ation is a universal one. There are 63,000 foreign doctors working in the United States and, in the Philippines, the authorities
had to hire a football stadium to seat all the doctors who
wanted to take American qualifying exams. In 1968, the
number of Filipino doctors going to America represented half
the output of Filipino medical schools.[7] One estimate says that
the number of Indian doctors working abroad is between 10
and 15,000, the same number that remain to serve a rural population of 450 million people.[8] The attractions that pull doctors
away from unappealing areas in the West and leave depleted
services are exactly the same attractions that pull Third World
doctors from the places in which they are needed and bring
them to us. The final losers on the chain are the rural populations of Asia, Africa and South America who attract nobody
but the dedicated or individualistic few to come and sort out
their problems.

Within the NHS they have been traditionally treated as a
labour force that can be relied on to do the jobs that British
doctors won't do. Their employment is part of a vicious circle
of deprivation and low prestige which keeps the most ambitious
British doctors out of certain areas, and keeps the most ambitious immigrant doctors in long-term jobs with little prospect
of transfer or promotion. Not only do these doctors get the most
thankless jobs in the long-stay hospitals, but they get them in
the least attractive geographical areas. If they set up in general
practice they are to be found, as often as not, in areas already
crowded with their compatriots, part of a sub-culture outside
the everyday framework of British society. If they work in hospitals while they gather qualifications to take home with them,
they have to do the jobs that no one else will take. David Owen,
as Minister of Health, estimated that in 1974 35% of hospital
doctors were foreign born, including 57% of registrars, 60% of
senior house officers and 28% of senior registrars.[9] But of this
35% a large proportion were heavily concentrated in certain
areas. 61% of senior registrars in geriatric medicine were immigrants and 70% of senior registrars in mental handicap. The
proportion was also higher in certain geographical areas. In

the West Midlands and North Yorkshire 40% of hospital doctors were immigrants, and in one of the large psychiatric hospitals on the periphery of London a consultant totted up his staff and found that eleven out of his thirteen junior doctors were foreign.

'As far as patients go, I lean on the nurses far more than I do on my foreign trained juniors who vary from quite good to bloody awful. I've got Bengalis, Punjabis, Indians, a Pakistani, an Egyptian. There's nothing you can do about the situation because of the shortage of British-trained doctors who gravitate to teaching hospitals or to good provincial hospitals. This situation is one of our greatest problems and it will only get worse because they now have to take an English test and the failure rate is alarming. The message will filter back home that it's not worthwhile investing all the money to come here. The doctors that I get here are really failed physicians and surgeons, and most of the work they do is not psychiatric. They're here to do simple medical work, treat bleeding and fractures and so on.'

In order to reduce these imbalances a more conscious effort is needed to attract doctors into the areas of work which they presently avoid and this effort should start very early. As long as so little attention is paid to the major problems of the health service in medical school curricula, and as long as the perfect medical career is seen to be one of advancement through the teaching hospitals, then young medical graduates will not be attracted to – or even informed about – the bulk of the work that faces the health service. If the gaps are to be stopped at all, the mechanisms which control medical ambitions will have to be radically altered. The pull of private practice in certain specialities and certain parts of the country will have to be counterbalanced by generous financial incentives for doctors who commit themselves full-time to the NHS. The merit award system should be abolished, and an open element of reward for service introduced to replace it which would make it a positive advantage to undertake unpopular work, rather than simply reinforce the attractions of acute medicine. If the shape of the service is to be altered to any significant degree and the problems in the care areas of health tackled, then young doctors mustn't feel that they are drifting into backwaters which may trap them for life. The element of a short-term service commitment which the Norwegians use so successfully would help to eliminate this fear and give more value to the caring function of medicine than it has at the present. Apart from tangible financial reward it is important, both for the individual doctor and for the speciality he represents, to keep doctors who undertake this kind of work in the mainstream of medicine. Professional stimulation and contact is almost more important than money. One suggestion is that teaching districts in the health service should adopt a deprived outlying district for the rotation of staff and the supply of just this stimulus and encouragement, and that consultants working in unattractive areas should be enticed by affiliation with a teaching hospital. This would not only ensure a continuous professional contact, but it would also bring the deprived areas of the health service to the notice of those – both teachers and students – who inhabit the teaching centres.

One area of the health service has always offered just this stimulation to doctors who might otherwise be working in isolation, and that is the health centre. When the health service was established the health centre was to be the basic building brick of primary care but somehow, over thirty years, it has never really got off the ground. Even now there are only 818 health centres in the country, and places which had been promised funding for health centres have real difficulty in finding doctors to staff them. One of the root causes of the comparative failure of the health centre concept is, again, the congenital independence of the medical profession. The general practitioner is an independent contractor and so, indeed, are the other health professionals who might staff a health centre, the opticians, dentists, pharmacists. As a single-handed practitioner, or even as a member of a group practice, he works from his own premises, but health centre premises belong to the health service and the whole concept of the health centre team brings the doctors nearer to the inauguration of a salaried service, something they resist quite fiercely. Some doctors also feel that as part of a health centre team they are in danger of losing that personal relationship with their own patients that is so important to them. Where health centres work they work well, and they seem to be a good answer to providing primary care in rural or in inner-city areas – the places where good general practice is thinnest on the ground. But as long as doctors see working in health centres as a threat to independence without any counter-balancing attractions of money or work, then there will continue to be difficulties in getting centres established.

There is an alternative approach to filling the gaps in the health service which involves a much more radical look at the medical role in health services, and a much more positive approach to using the skills of other health workers. Although barefoot doctors as such are inappropriate to an industrialized society, it is still worth considering a reappraisal of the use of skills within the health service. Because of the areas of medical emptiness left by the world migrations of nomadic doctors, those people who concern themselves with the problems of rural poverty and neglected populations have come up with a variety of solutions along the same lines. If the traditional concept of the scientifically trained hospital doctor is inapplicable, or at least impractical, for the problems in hand, then a new kind of health worker is needed, one who can be trained to perform simple medical tasks which cover a basic range of health problems and which don't take years to learn, and one, most important of all, who will be at home in the population which he or she serves. The *feldsher* in Russia, the barefoot doctor in China, the physician's assistant in the United States, the nurse-practitioner in Canada are all filling gaps which the most advanced and expensive kinds of medicine are proving unsuited to stopping, and helping to make more rational use of specialized and sophisticated medical manpower.

Through television and the newspapers we follow this kind of development with remote interest but the lessons that it has for the NHS could be valuable. It is quite clear that we are failing to cope with all the problems that present themselves. Maybe our whole concept of what health care should be and the kind of personnel who should deliver it need re-examining in the light of a more basic approach. Maybe we could get more health care for our money if doctors relinquished their hold on procedures which many other workers in the health service are capable of doing. Family planning is a case in point. Only doctors are authorized to prescribe the contraceptive pill, though in many cases the examinations they carry out and the controls they exercise are minimal to non-existent. Doctors are so far the only people authorized to fit intra-uterine devices although one hospital has experimented with allowing nurses to carry out this procedure. All that nurses are generally allowed to do is fit Dutch caps. And since 1975, the government has decided to make extra payments to doctors carrying out certain contraceptive procedures, notably sterilization and the fitting of intra-uterine devices in hospitals – a payment which some doctors have refused to accept. Now, in poorer countries, all these tasks have proved to be well within the competence of people who are not only medically unqualified, but are even illiterate. The most celebrated example of this delegation of a medical task is the WHO (World Health Organization) sponsored project in Bangladesh where illiterate village women were taught to carry out the simple surgical operation of sterilization by tubal ligation.[10] Not only did they prove perfectly capable of carrying out the procedure but the results of their work, undertaken in primitive village conditions, compared favourably for competence and conditions of sterility with the same operation conducted in a hospital. It is significant that hostility to this project came from within the local medical profession, and not from the project workers or the village women themselves – in fact one of the workers was murdered and the local doctor was charged with the crime.

In countries like Bangladesh this solution, or something like it, to the problems of providing basic health care to a large impoverished population is widely accepted. But we have no particular reason to be smug. It is not inappropriate, given our patent failure to meet demand, to look at our own problems with a low-level solution in mind. In almost every country in the West, the idea that the hospital doctor, with his six years of basic training and a further lifetime of specialization, is the only person qualified to cope with health problems is being questioned. The problem is most urgent where this paragon simply fails to appear. In the United States where some of the best, the most sophisticated, the most technological health care in the world is applied, there are areas where doctors are very thin on the ground. In 1974, thirty-three states authorized the presence of a grade called the physician's assistant and seven authorized nurse-practitioners.[11] The principle behind physician's assistants is that they should extend the effectiveness of the physician by taking over routine work, and freeing the doctor, both to concentrate on work which actually demands his training and skills, and also to continue this training by taking up further study and education. The use of physician's assistants also extends the primary health care team. In the United States it costs ten times as much to train a doctor as to train a nurse, and yet an increasing number of studies in Britain and North America are producing evidence that nurses are just as competent, and as acceptable to patients as doctors, in coping with the majority of complaints which present themselves to the average family surgery or health centre. The most famous study, the *Burlington randomized trial of the nurse-practitioner* in Canada, showed that when a qualified nurse and a general practitioner shared a normal general practice, the nurse was perfectly capable of dealing with 90% of the problems which came to the surgery. And, what is more, that the patients were perfectly satisfied with the nurse's care.[12] A training programme for nurse-practitioners at McMaster University in Canada aims to give nurses the skill and confidence to make independent clinical judgements and act upon them. It has already trained ninety-nine nurse-practitioners to undertake routine medical work like family planning, the management of overweight and hypertensive patients, antenatal care and routine examinations. The graduates of this programme have found that they are doing twice as much clinical work as they did before and only half as much administration, while the doctors with whom they work find that they are released to spend more time with patients who really need a doctor's attention. The increase in professional satisfaction, and in efficient use of professional skills and time, works both ways.

The primary care system in Britain needs just such a fresh look. A study carried out in Scotland under the aegis of the Royal College of General Practitioners showed that in 1000 representative episodes of illness during working hours in a large electrical company in Edinburgh, the two nurses on duty were quite capable of dealing with between 95% and 97·5% without any further reference to a doctor.[13] In only 2·5% of cases was any further action by a doctor necessary. This unrecognized competence of the lower trained worker to do the work of the more highly trained spreads itself into hospital medicine. Another study carried out in hospital casualty departments showed that 70% of the work was within the competence of the nurse. If you ask, 'then why don't they do it?', particularly considering the intolerable waits often forced upon patients in casualty departments while they wait for some harassed doctor to materialize, the answer is partly professional demarcation, but more commonly the real fear of legal responsibility, and the ever-present threat of legal action should anything go wrong. It is interesting to look at the point made by advocates of physician's assistants in the States that their use would tend to reduce rather than increase the threat of malpractice, since malpractice suits result far more from bad communication with patients than from actual incompetence. The efficient use of auxiliary help in medical care ought to mean that the patient is seen more quickly and more competently, and that the chances of the harassed, delayed consultation are reduced.

The Canadian experience is perfectly applicable to Britain as a few facts will show. Two thirds of British general practices employ nurses, but in the most boring and inefficient way. Whereas the average thirty-seven-hour week of the nurse-practitioner is spent on 70% clinical work with patients, half of the average twenty-three-hour week of the British general practice nurse is spent on purely administrative and secretarial duties which need no qualifications, and which can't be as satisfying as direct patient work. Part of the fault lies in the traditional way in which doctors and nurses see their role. Despite the evidence that nurses and low-grade health workers are capable of much more than is demanded of them, a survey of doctors' and nurses' attitudes to work showed that both professions thought that nurses would only be capable of doing about 20% of the doctors' work. And yet an American paediatric practice reported that a paediatric nurse-practitioner employed by them was responsible for a great range of clinical work, including the supervision of other workers in the practice, the counselling of parents, the conduction of examinations and screening tests on the patients.[14]

There is another aspect to the use of lower level health workers which is not simply to save money by the efficient use of cheaper skills, and that is the use of local skills in areas which don't attract doctors. Rather than expecting doctors to work in unattractive areas, both medical and geographical, it may be a sensible alternative solution to retrain those workers already there to undertake more responsible work. This already applies in certain areas – for example, nurses in the psychiatric and geriatric services already carry a great deal of responsibility simply because doctors are so few and far between, and the day-to-day management of patients has to be left in their care. An up-grading of the most competent nursing staff into nurse-therapists would improve the service, relieve some of the pressure on medical staff and give a professional boost to the nursing profession already involved. A solution to the problems of maldistribution of medical care lies in a close look at the role of the doctor and in the proper use of his abilities and training, along with a fresh look at the potential of other workers in the health service. In the future the health services may get the best bargain – and the patients receive the best care – from a medical team in which the doctor used his skills and knowledge in a much more managerial role, while other staff take much more of the load of routine work off his desk.

6   Yes – But Does It Work?

There is a verifiable rule in modern health services, a kind of self-fulfilling prophecy which says that health care workers, and in particular doctors, will do what they have been taught to do regardless of other considerations. An American health economist has neatly tagged this natural phenomenon as 'the technological imperative', the desire of the physician to do everything he has been trained to do regardless of cost and, as we shall see, regardless of proven benefit. The director general of the World Health Organization, Dr Halfdan Mahler, summed it up by saying

health care workers consider that the best health care is one where everything known to medicine is applied to every individual by the highest trained medical scientist in the most specialized institution. It is frightening, but expected, that when a specialist group is formed to perform certain actions it is evaluated and continues to be supported because of the number of such actions which are done, rather than whether the problem is solved.

As a consequence doctors commit health services to vast amounts of expenditure over which very little control has been exercised. In his book *Who Shall Live?*, American health economist Victor Fuchs quotes a Dr Paul Elwood, who points out succinctly that, 'Hospitals don't have patients. Doctors have patients, and hospitals have doctors.'[1] As a consequence, Fuchs adds, 'from the point of view of the hospital administrator, running a hospital is like trying to drive a car when the passengers have control of the wheel and the accelerator. The most the administrator can do is occasionally jam on the brakes'. The combination of individual clinical freedom for the doctor with the enormous potential of modern medicine has brought about a state of medical inflation. Medical inflation could be controlled by some kind of government intervention or by raising

D

the consciousness of the patient so that we all become less demanding, but in the long run it is the doctor who controls the purse-strings. No government can interfere with totalitarian ruthlessness between doctor and patient, and however demanding a patient it is his doctor who decides whether or not to go ahead with treatment. This chapter is concerned with the growing need for the medical profession itself to monitor its own activities in the interests of a more efficient health service.

It is doctors who prescribe drugs, order tests, admit patients, perform operations, decide how long patients should stay in hospital. The technological imperative encourages them in a habit of intervention which, in the long run, may be good for neither doctor nor patient. Every doctor will acknowledge that most illnesses run a natural course at the end of which most patients get better. Many diseases which do not are incurable. And yet the pattern of intervention grows. In the United States, twenty-five million operations are performed each year, and during the 1970s the number of operations performed rose by 23%, while the population only grew by 5%. Even the American College of Surgeons and the American Surgical Association admit that there are 30% more practising surgeons in the United States than are strictly necessary.[2] In America too, where the system of payment and the growing habit of suing doctors encourages even more interventive medicine than in Europe, the number of babies delivered by caesarian section has risen sharply in recent years, partly because obstetricians have chosen to operate if foetal monitoring indicates any kind of trouble. And yet caesarian section is by no means the safest way to deliver a child, and American obstetricians have produced no conclusive evidence that children delivered by caesarian section are better off than children delivered normally, or by a forceps delivery. It is a classic case of using a technique because it is there and because it makes medicine look busier.

This same desire to zap the patient with modern technology can be shown to act positively against the patient's interests. In 1975, over 40% of American hospitals with fewer than 100 beds had intensive care units, and in the same year 91 hospitals in

California were performing cardiac surgery.[3] The element of commercial competition and lack of overall coordination in the American health system encourages this kind of duplication, but even within the NHS the demands of consultants produce a similar situation. Eighteen London hospitals undertake open heart surgery and in 1965, 45 hospitals were equipped to do pacemaker implants of which 10 did only one a year.[4] The safest unit to be in for a complicated operation is the one which carries out that operation most frequently. The chances of killing your patients are statistically higher if you only carry out five such operations a year than if you carry out fifty. One argument for the heavy provision of the more spectacular techniques in teaching hospitals is that students need to learn in the units, but given the very high cost of equipping special units, and the expert staff needed to run them, and the laboratories needed to serve them, there is a strong need for even more centralization and shared facilities.

The clearest and most eloquent voice for self-control within the medical profession was raised in 1971 when Professor A. L. Cochrane produced his elegant essay on *Effectiveness and Efficiency: Random Reflections on Health Services*.[5] Cochrane was summarizing previous work that had been done in the evaluation of medical procedures, and making a succinct plea for a more scientific attitude to medicine in the future in the interests of a more rational health service. 'I once,' wrote Cochrane, 'asked a worker in a crematorium who had a curiously contented look on his face, what he found so satisfying about his work. He replied that what fascinated him was the way in which so much went in and so little came out. I thought of advising him to get a job with the NHS, it might have increased his job satisfaction.'

Cochrane's case is that the NHS will never be as good as it could be until we are 'able to express the results in the form of the benefit and the cost to the population of a particular type of activity, and the increased benefit that could be obtained if more money were made available'. In order to do this, we have to be able to measure the effect of treatment on the course of an illness and also decide whether all the vast forces of the NHS are wisely and efficiently brought to bear in carrying out the treatment. The assumption behind this approach is that a great deal of medicine is of no scientifically proven value at all – even techniques which are widely in use. What Cochrane and his followers ask is that new therapies, and old but questionable therapies, be strictly and scientifically tested rather than absorbed unquestioningly into the health service armoury. No commercial organization, they point out, would preside over so enormous a budget as the National Health Service's without a research section checking on whether the budget was wisely spent.

The technique most widely used for the evaluation of medical therapy is the Randomized Controlled Trial, a simple technique which involves the use of two groups of patients randomly chosen and even, when applicable, a double blind by which not even the doctor knows which patient is getting the placebo and which the active therapy. Unfortunately not all procedures are suitable for this kind of evaluation, and some doctors raise the question of ethics – is it right to deny a patient a potentially successful treatment for the sake of a scientific test? One instance where the RCT (Randomized Controlled Trial) has never been applied – although Cochrane thinks it ought to be – is the use of smear tests to detect cervical cancer in women, a screening procedure which most women gratefully undergo. But is it really effective in reducing the death rate from cervical cancer? Cochrane has his doubts.

The death rate for carcinoma of the cervix was falling before smears were introduced and has continued to fall at roughly the same rate in most areas. No convincing evidence has been published of a greater fall of this death rate in areas where there has been a high coverage of the female population when compared with similar areas where little such work has been done . . . it appears to me still possible that smears may have some preventive effect, but we may never know, and the health services of the world may well expend thousands of millions of pounds in the hope of preventing a relatively rare though severe condition whose mortality rate is decreasing fairly rapidly.

Professor Cochrane divides the failings of the health service into two main groups – the use of ineffective therapies, and the use of effective therapies at the wrong time, as, for example, in useless tonics which still contain ingredients which might be effective in other circumstances and other bottles. Likewise a treatment may be effective but if it is given in the wrong place – a hospital ward, say, when it could be administered in out patients or at home – it becomes inefficient, or a hospital stay which is justified may become inefficient if it goes on too long. There are many examples of trials on therapies or procedures which have effectively altered attitudes and consequently medical practice.

One of the most famous examples in recent years is the trial set up by the Department of Health and Social Security into the value of high-technology coronary units.[6] Coronary care units (CCUs) with their battery of machines and their intensive surveillance with monitors represent the acme of technological medicine. Their patients lie plugged in to a variety of incomprehensible machines and screens, and their life-line is reduced to an electronic signal bleeping across the screen like a TV tennis game. The study examined the recovery rate of heart patients in these very expensive units compared with heart patients who were simply tended at home. The doctors involved were not at all happy about the ethics of this particular trial, suspecting naturally that the patients who were being nursed at home were being denied possibly invaluable care and therefore used unethically. As the results emerged, it began to look as though the patients at home had a rather better survival rate than those who were receiving the best of technological medicine. To tease the doctors the researchers told them at first that the trial had proved that the patients in the CCUs were doing better than the ones at home. Outraged, the doctors declared the trial unethical and demanded that the patients who were at home be brought into the safety of the hospital. When they were told the true results, that the death rate was higher in a coronary care unit than at home, there was a great deal of very heated debate, but no suggestion was made to close down the coronary care units. A more recent trial, whose results were published in 1977, pointed out that despite the introduction of coronary care units into Britain over the last ten years, the death rate from heart attacks has been unaffected. This trial found no significant difference in the recovery rate of patients nursed in coronary care units and in the normal medical ward.

Another procedure that has enjoyed a great vogue in recent years is the intricate wizardry of the coronary by-pass operation, in which vein grafts from the patient's leg or groin are sewn into the coronary arteries to permit blood to flow round the areas which have become clogged by etherosclerosis. The alternative treatment for angina pectoris is the use of powerful drugs, and by-pass surgery seemed, for a time, to offer the answer. Waiting lists for by-pass surgery grew and it became an international commodity as patients from Europe who couldn't get it done at home or who had to wait too long, flew to hospitals in America and Britain to get their operations performed. But a recent medical study carried out in thirteen Veterans' Administration hospitals in the United States showed no significant difference in the survival rate of angina patients undergoing surgery and those undergoing treatment by drugs.[7] The same percentage in each group – 88% – were alive after three years. The findings of this study have been bitterly disputed by many surgeons, but it is a good illustration of the critical function of a properly conducted study or trail in questioning procedures that can easily become fashionable, then routine, overnight.

One routine operation that is so commonly conducted that no member of the public thinks of it as hazardous or questionable is tonsillectomy. And yet trials done on tonsillectomy have shown how inapplicable and unnecessary it is in many cases and have reduced the number of operations done. In Britain tonsillectomy is the commonest cause of admission to hospital for children, and it currently accounts for over 150,000 admissions to hospital each year.[8] Tonsillectomy in the past has been considered as a kind of cure-all for childhood complaints, even though no operation involving general anaesthesia is free from risk. Nowadays the criteria for admitting a child for tonsillectomy are much tighter and it is generally agreed that it is only really effective when it is needed to relieve obstruction of the airways. Three trials into the effectiveness of tonsillectomy in Britain seems to confirm rather than disprove the value of the operation, but the trials themselves were not perfectly designed to be free of bias. In the United States, where all surgical procedures have increased dramatically, tonsillectomy is one of the very few to show a decrease because of a study in the Children's Hospital of Pittsburgh which found that only 8% of tonsillectomies were clearly medically justified.[9] As a consequence the rate of tonsillectomy in America has dropped by 41·11% in five years. It is estimated that if all cases in Britain were first referred for medical treatment and only later sent for surgery, the rate of the operation could be cut to one-fifth of its present numbers.

In another case where doctors stood back and re-evaluated their use of technology for technology's sake, they questioned the automatic use of incubators for new born babies except under certain well-defined conditions. The paediatric unit at Addenbrooke's Hospital, Cambridge, used to have a blanket policy of incubating – and thus separating from their mothers at a crucial time – all babies who weighed under 2·4 kilos at birth, all babies delivered by forceps, all babies delivered by caesarian section. They then set up a trial to see what happened when only the really ill babies were put in the incubators and the rest were left in the care of their mothers on the wards. They found that the babies who stayed with their mothers did just as well without incubation which is, in any case, a separation which can present real problems to the forming of the mother and child bond, as well as using expensive equipment inefficiently. It was estimated, on the basis of this study, that if this selective policy were adopted nationwide, up to 50,000 babies annually could stay with their mothers at this crucial period of their life.

But the potentialities of technological medicine are far from being the only aspect of medical care that benefit from a close, scientific scrutiny. There is no consensus of opinion on how long a patient should stay in hospital for any given procedure although the variations from doctor to doctor, from region to region, must account for very large sums of money in the use of hospital facilities. Studies have shown that 25–30% of hospital patients needn't be there at all from the point of view of requiring the special care that a hospital offers. Patients themselves wonder sometimes if it is really necessary for them to go in so early, and more and more studies are aimed at finding out if it is necessary for them to be there so long. Certain common reasons for admittance such as childbirth, have shrunk from a regulation ten days to a swift forty-eight hours. Varicose veins can take a week of hospital time in one place and twenty-four hours in another. David Ennals estimated in a speech that if all hospital stays longer than the average were cut back to the average £26 million would be saved. Beds in hospitals are not a Good Thing in the sense that if we only had more beds, waiting lists would disappear and all our problems would be solved. A study of 177 large hospitals showed that both admissions to hospital and length of stay increased according to the availability of beds – a Parkinson's Law of health in which patients expand to fill the beds available.[10] In other words there is no ideal capacity at which hospital waiting lists would start going down.

And even the simple notion of bed rest itself is something that can be questioned. Most of us assume that whatever surgery or drugs might do to you, bed rest is the lowest common denominator of good medical care. Bed rest in hospital under medical supervision and nursing care can surely do you nothing but good, but we take it too much for granted. A famous study undertaken by the World Health Organization into the treatment of pulmonary tuberculosis over five years showed that even in the poorest areas of Madras in India, there was absolutely no difference in the rate of recovery between TB patients under medical observation in hospitals, and patients who were simply treated at home.[11] It is not so long ago that the treatment of pulmonary tuberculosis automatically meant weeks, even months, of enforced restrictive bed rest – as Betty Macdonald's book *The Plague and I* chronicled, minute by frustrating minute, but other studies than the WHO project have shown it to be unnecessary. In fact the reduction of the destructive power of TB from an often terminal to an easily treatable disease, owes a great deal to the use of RCTs in establishing effective treatment and drug dosages.

The whole question of evaluation and cost-effectiveness in medicine rises most aggressively in the area of drug usage and prescription. The pressure for some kind of control of the drug industry, of the effects of individual drugs, of prescribing costs, of prescribing habits is continual from many quarters, and compared with many other countries Britain is lucky to have a centralized government-controlled health service that can have some control over prices, drug safety and over-prescribing, but very few people would dispute that there is a very long way to go yet. Prescription of drugs is a hit-and-miss business which cost the country £451 million in 1976. In 1949 the NHS drug bill was only £39 million and yet the actual number of annual prescriptions has increased by only one-fifth. Over half of the annual expenditure associated with the GP is accounted for by the drugs which he prescribes at an average cost per prescription of £1·30. The charging of a prescription fee to the patient, which stands at 45p at the moment, has failed to save money since the doctor has simply responded by increasing the amount prescribed each time, and in consequence unswallowed antibiotics alone cost the NHS over £5 million at the last count. Before prescription charges, as one doctor explained, he would prescribe just the necessary dose for a patient which might be no more than three tablets. Now that the patient has to pay, he or she objects to receiving such a minute dose for his money, so the doctor compensates by over-prescribing.

The larger part of the drugs which we collect from the chemist, swallowed or not, are not to effect dramatic life-and-death cures or to relieve great pain. The very high prescribing of psychotropic drugs reflects the family doctor's way of coping with a growing work-load which is either openly psychological in origin, or which he suspects might be. He simply doesn't have the time to spend talking his patients' problems through with them, or the power to change their life-style into something less stressful so he prescribes instead, and the patient goes to the doctor with the expectation that he will prescribe. A bottle of medicine, a jar of pills are the concrete symbol of the transaction between doctor and patient and we feel cheated if we don't get it. Medicine is passive. It requires no further effort from us except to take it, and being on some kind of drug from the doctor is a sort of badge of identity. For the doctor, the proliferation of new drugs and treatments offers a great scope of alternatives. If one thing doesn't work, then he can try another, and the pulling out of the pen and the prescription pad marks a satisfactory end to a consultation, though the quantity of unconsumed drugs is some indication that patients as well as doctors, are aware of its purely symbolic nature. Richard Gordon wrote in *Punch* that:

The family doctor, faced every surgery with one sick patient for five perfectly fit ones, cooperates by readily jotting a prescription as an alternative to three-quarters of an hour on the patient's sexual fantasies, always overwhelmingly uninteresting. As doctors are laughingly expected to prescribe only for diseases, the GP accepts the drug salesman's whisper that the wretched patient suffers from 'psychic tension', or 'subliminal anxiety'. The drug firm, having invented new diseases, applies itself not to their eradication but to their promotion.

And the drug companies try very hard. According to the Association of the British Pharmaceutical Industry, 13% of its total sales revenue to the NHS goes on promotion to doctors. In 1974, these sales totalled £287 million, which makes the promotion budget of the British drug industry alone nearly £40 million, or an average of £500 per year per doctor. From the moment a schoolboy or schoolgirl becomes a medical student, he or she becomes the object of lavish attentions from the drug industry which ceases only with retirement or death. New controls induced by the government aim at reducing the proportion of profits spent on promotion to 10% by 1979 and have restricted the distribution of gifts and samples and the lavish hospitality which doctors have traditionally enjoyed. According to one estimate, more is spent on drug advertising to each doctor over his working life than it costs the state to train him in the first place, and for the cost of the sales promotion aimed at him by the drug companies, says another estimate, it would be possible for each GP to have a highly qualified medical specialist spend one month a year retraining him.

The bulk of this promotion, which comes to him through medical journals, through direct mail of samples and brochures through his letter-box, through personal visits from drug company salesmen and women – young, pretty women are increasingly popular – from lavish entertaining in hospitals, universities and medical conferences, is aimed, not so much at giving him better information as to what the forty or so new products advertised each year can do, but to instil a brand preference into him. In the United States this industry is even more prodigal – American drug companies employ over 20,000 salesmen to visit doctors and spend an average of 4,000 dollars each year on each doctor.[12] Surveys conducted into the effect of all this promotion show that while the average doctor recognizes the efficiency of the industry in telling him what is new on the market, he prefers to rely on the medical journals and on his peers to tell him how effective the product is. He recognizes that, one way or the other, he needs some guidance. The world market for pharmaceuticals is expected to reach £20,000 million by 1980 and it covers thousands of registered products, many of which are near duplicates, or very minor variations, of drugs which already exist.

It would be quite wrong to imply that the drug industry is an evil business which exists only to make enormous sums of money. All of us have a great deal to be very thankful for in the efficiency of modern medicines, and mortality for a great many once common conditions has dropped dramatically during this century, thanks to drugs. One estimate says that our economy profits by £55 million each year because of the use of modern anti-tuberculous drugs. Another points out that deaths from gastro-intestinal infections have dropped 80% in fifty years, deaths from lung infections by 70%.[13] Antibiotics, psychotropic drugs, above all the contraceptive pill – the most widely taken drug in Britain – have transformed the quality of life. And yet there is still a need for controls. We need controls over the cost of drugs, over their safety, over their prescribing and over their use. Some of these controls already exist. Britain has the cheapest drugs of any of the developed countries, thanks to the existence of the NHS and the government as a monopoly buyer. The profitability of the drug industry has fallen from 27·2% on capital in 1967 to 14·7% in 1974, and this has come about partly because of the controls of the NHS. This fact offers hope to other countries who are moving towards more state control of medicine. An Officer of Health Economics publication points out that 'it is at least fairly safe to conclude that by the end of the century social security schemes of one kind or another providing medical care for everyone will be universal in civilized countries when in consequence the state will everywhere have become the chief customer of the (drug) industry'. A powerful buyer like a government can even fight back at what it considers to be undue profiteering, as in the famous case in which the British government sued the Swiss drug firm of Hoffman La Roche over its giant profits on Valium and Librium, and won. It is worth noting that export prices of British drugs are about twice the price paid by the NHS.

Controls on safety also exist, although those that escape the net become notorious. Even the most effective drugs can have unpleasant side-effects, and the wrong use of a drug, its overuse, or its use with some incompatible substance or its use at the wrong time, can lead to serious symptoms of illness or damage. The case of thalidomide use in pregnancy is the obvious example, but there is current concern over the use of beta blockers in the treatment of heart disease. Doctors are supposed to report possible side-effects of drugs to the Committee on Safety of Medicines, with the help of a yellow report card, a system which is generally satisfactory. However, in the case of Eraldin, a beta blocking agent, only one doctor reported any adverse side-effects – damage to the eye – by the time 100,000 patients had taken the drug. After this was reported, more than

200 earlier cases of eye damage came to light, and two cases where major surgery was required. The drug was withdrawn, and the use of beta blockers has come under more intensive examination.[14]

Such controls as do exist over the prescribing habits of individual doctors tend to be rather toothless, and to concentrate more on the quantity of drug prescribed than on the quality. In 1972, for example, 3,035 contacts were made by health service officials to over-prescribing doctors and only in one case was further action taken. Doctors often regard this as a horrid interference in their business and in their clinical freedom, and yet where individual practices have taken steps to control their own prescribing they can achieve encouraging results. Two letters from doctors to the *British Medical Journal* pointed out that they were quite capable of controlling costs – and of achieving a better understanding of their patients – by reducing their number of prescriptions. One pointed out that 'in my own practice in 1959 my costs were 80% of average and yearly that figure was reduced to 20% as I understood more the nature of consultations and got to know patients ... educating the patient clarifies the situation ... thus I find that prescribing frequency and work-load diminish in parallel and educating and prescribing have an inverse relationship'. The other doctor made more concrete suggestions for encouraging doctors to reduce prescribing. 'I propose that any practitioner whose prescribing costs per head fall below 80% of the area average for four consecutive years should have the chance to claim the percentage saving of one year for reinvestment in his practice, subject to appropriate safeguards. For twenty-three years the cost of prescribing in this practice has not been above 75% of the area average ... over a period of twelve months our practice has saved at least £21,420 compared with the average cost of prescribing for a similar number of patients. Some part of these savings should come back to us to be reinvested for the benefit of our patients. This would at once encourage thrift and improve our facilities.'

Where doctors work together in a group practice or health

centre they have the advantage of comparing notes with colleagues, and they can work together to adopt a systematic approach to prescribing rather than the automatic repeat prescription and the placebo. One South Wales practice found that by approaching a particular medical problem logically, it was able to reduce costs even though the drugs in question were expensive ones. 'We were worried about our prescribing costs because we had started to use expensive beta blockers for hypertension. We had a look at the practice expenditure on cardiovascular drugs and we found – despite our having found and treated every hypertensive patient in the practice who needed treatment – that our costs were 20% below average for Glamorgan as a whole, and 83% below average for drugs acting on the cardiovascular system. The answer seemed to be that we were not treating patients who did not warrant treatment on our criteria. We had abolished treatment with one tablet of what have you three times a day without any definite control.'

The single-handed GP is in a much more vulnerable position as regards the bewildering world of pharmaceuticals. There has been such an explosion in the research, production and high pressure marketing of new or renamed drugs that no individual doctor can possibly hope to keep usefully abreast of what is effective and what is not. Because of this problem the best hope for informed and economical prescribing in the future may lie in a liaison of the individual doctor with more specialized colleagues in the health service, through a strong programme of continuing education for doctors in drug use, through alliance with specialized drug information units, and through a closer partnership with his neglected colleague, the pharmacist. Continuing education in drug information is vital for the doctor, whatever his speciality. Some critics of the present system claim that wiser prescribing should start with the medical school curriculum where, too often, pharmacology has been taught as a pre-clinical science and not as a clinical discipline involving actual patients. Once the doctor has left medical school his information on drugs comes to him largely via the drug companies as well as through the medical journals, but although drug companies play a valuable part in informing doctors about their products, it could be convincingly argued that information and education of this kind should not be left to organizations with such a strong commercial interest, but should be taken over by the NHS itself, or by some independent educational organization.

In future there may be more room for units like the clinical drug information service run in the Northern Region which provides a twenty-four-hour service run by eight doctors to provide their medical colleagues within the region with clinical information and advice.[15] At the moment there is only one such unit, but they estimate that with a large enough team on call, the service could be run without interfering with the other research, clinical and teaching commitments of the doctors concerned. But while such services are thin on the ground, doctors have easy access to another profession whose particular expertise is drugs – the pharmacist. With the rise in popularity of brand-name drugs the role of the pharmacist as drug dispenser has dwindled to that of a highly trained shopkeeper, but the growth of the pharmaceutical industry could equally well supply him with a new role as the specialized adviser of the doctor on the properties of new drugs coming on to the market. The pharmacist already fulfils a very useful role as one of the front-line people in primary care, and could offer more expert help to the public without warping the doctor's role. The pharmacist is also valuable in that the drugs bought directly from him by the public without a prescription are more assiduously taken than those prescribed for them by a doctor. If necessary, the training of the pharmacist could be biased in future towards giving primary care and advice as well as serving as a drug information service to local doctors.

There is another controllable factor in the exchange of drugs, by no means the least important, and that is the patient. The vast pharmaceutical industry, the millions of pounds, the thousands of products would not be generated if there were not a huge and seemingly insatiable demand from the public for drugs for every possible occasion. The world record for the consumption of drugs is still held, as far as anyone knows, by one Samuel Jessup, a Lincolnshire grazier who, between the years 1794 and 1816 managed to swallow 226,934 tablets washed down by 40,000 bottles of medicine, and was thus recorded for posterity as a phenomenon. But it is far from uncommon for patients today to get through as many pills per day as he did – it works out at nearly 30 a day. In Britain, and in societies even more drug-oriented than ours, a strong pressure comes from the patient to prescribe. A doctor writing from Chicago pointed out that 'writing prescriptions helps to terminate the interview, make up for lack of time, mollifies the chronic complainer and provides an adequate supply for diversion to those who occasionally, or continuously, need to feel high . . . to deny a patient his expected shot of penicillin requires unusual fortitude and scientific detachment – and the same goes for his sleeping pills, tranquillizers and analgesics, his hormones, multi-vitamins and tonic injections – not to speak of self-administered laxatives, sinus drops, brewer's yeast and vitamin E'.

The unhappy effects of over, or unwise, prescribing are seen at their worst among old people. It is not uncommon for them to end up with a score of little bottles at their bedside and to become hopelessly confused as to what they are supposed to take and why. They become confused as a result of taking the drugs as well; the combination of so many chemicals with an ageing body often results in drug-induced symptoms of senile dementia and extreme confusion which can sometimes be cured simply by withdrawing medication. This is an extremely serious problem which is exacerbated by the growing attention being paid to the large market presented to the drug companies by the ageing population. The glossier medical journals are full of smiling grannies and active grandads advertising the benefits of a whole range of drugs aimed at the ailments of old age. No wonder that so many of them suffer from what one doctor labelled 'the shopping bag syndrome' after he looked into the shopping bag of an old lady leaving hospital and found her carrying thirteen different drugs. One American study found that hospital patients receive an average of eight different drugs per hospital admission and another, at Johns Hopkins Hospital, Baltimore, found that the average number of medicines consumed while the patient was in hospital was fourteen – the highest was thirty-two.

The ill effects of this vast consumption work in two basically opposing ways – the danger of overdose and the dangers of underdose. On the one hand patients take far too many drugs and fall victim either to deliberate self-poisoning, or to iatrogenic disease. On the other, patients abuse drugs by taking them at the wrong time, in the wrong order, failing to finish a course prescribed, failing to collect or take their prescriptions, failing, as the jargon has it, to 'comply'. The hoarded jars and bottles and tubes in every British home are just as much an abuse of drugs and of NHS resources as the overdoses that end up in the casualty ward on a Saturday night. On the one hand an investigation into 500 households in Hartlepool found 43,000 unused tablets – a figure which represented one and a quarter billion unused items in the country as a whole at a cost to the NHS of £6,500,000.[16] On the other hand, self-poisoning is the second most common cause of emergency admission to hospital. Each year nearly 3,000 people die in England and Wales as a direct result of drug overdose and the rate of iatrogenic disease is estimated at between 10 and 15%.

Over three hundred papers dealing with the problems of compliance with doctors' orders and prescriptions have been written in the English language in the last fifteen years, and it seems that the most important factor in the sensible and economic use of drugs by the public is the relationship between the public and the doctor.[17] It comes right back to the prescription pad on the GP's desk and the way in which the individual doctor communicates with the individual patient. A study in Nottingham on the effects of counselling on compliance found that any kind of memory aid, such as calendars or pill wheels, was ineffective compared with fifteen minutes spent by the doctor in explaining carefully what the patient had to do.[18] The patients who had this counselling made less than a third of the errors made by

E

those who hadn't. Wherever one looks in the tangle of problems presented by efforts to control supply and demand in the health service, the power for change and therefore the ultimate responsibility lies with the medical profession.

It is a responsibility which the medical profession should welcome rather than evade. It is all too clear that, given the problem of world-wide medical inflation, control must either come from within, or be imposed from without, and yet the medical profession, despite its conservatism and resistance to interference, also has an honourable tradition of self-analysis and soul-searching. Attendance at a medical conference can be a revelation in the ruthless sniping, the no-holds-barred criticism between colleagues, and at least one branch of medicine has made a regular habit of critical analysis and record keeping, with excellent results for its patients. In the interests of keeping more mothers and babies alive and healthy, obstetricians have shown more aptitude for self-criticism and limitation of clinical freedom in the general interest than some of their colleagues in other branches of medicine. The first *Report on Confidential Enquiries into Maternal Deaths in England and Wales* appeared in 1952, and the exercise has been carried out regularly ever since. Even by 1962, the Department of Health was able to call the report 'a unique exercise in medicine in this country – a careful review . . . in an attempt to ascertain whether additional or different action . . . might have given the patient a better prospect of survival . . . to derive lessons'. It is worth noting that under this close scrutiny one of the major lessons is that in many cases the woman herself was responsible for the dangerous conditions of her labour and consequent death, simply through ignoring the advice of her doctors and taking no antenatal care.

Another move in the same self-critical direction has been taken by the Scottish Home and Health Department which attempts to initiate this kind of inquiry and comparison by sending out to all consultants in the health service a regular statistical report on the patients treated by him, and comparative figures on the patients treated by his colleagues in the same speciality and region. The need for close self-examination of this kind is pointed up by another survey which found that within two years of leaving hospital, over a third of all patients were dead, and over half of them if not dead were unimproved. If hospital care makes so little difference, then doctors should look at what they do with a fresh eye – unlike the consultants in the Oxford Region who, in a survey, were found to have no idea whether or not their patients had died on discharge.

And yet, despite precedents and examples in other countries, many doctors are deeply concerned about the threat to their independence of judgement and action offered by interference in their work in the wider interests of a rational health service. A recent commentary in the *British Medical Journal* looked at the current situation in Sweden and Malta and quotes the prestigious *New England Journal of Medicine* as saying:

government control will increasingly encompass the practice of medicine and the course of scientific research. This process has been nurtured, perhaps unwittingly, by health professionals, chiefly of academic origin, and a few from labour unions, who would put medicine and research under the hegemony of legislators, planners and consumers and lawyers to form a 'health care industry' and 'science for the people'.

'Why,' asks the *BMJ* commentator, 'should this idea be so repugnant to doctors and why should their independence be so precious to them?' His answer is that a 'liberally educated, inquiring, professional individual, trained to act decisively, is or should be the patients' best protection against the clumsy and impersonal procedures of the state'. He fails to ask the reverse question. Who is the patients' best protection against the clumsy and highly personal procedures of the doctor? The answer should be – and there are encouraging signs that it will be – other doctors. There is plenty of encouragement in this direction from other countries. In Denmark and New Zealand medical committees operate to examine and recommend preferred drugs, and there seems to be no reason why this system should not work in Britain. In America, which has had a stronger tradition of medical audit than we have up till now, it is common practice for hospital doctors to conduct communal post-mortems on failed cases, and most hospitals have tissue committees that review specimens after an operation to make sure that the operation was justified. In a further attempt to control the inflationary rate of surgery in the United States, the medical profession is organizing itself into Professional Standards Review Organizations to monitor medical treatment and surgery that is covered by Medicare and Medicaid. An additional incentive could be offered to doctors to cooperate in their own self-control by offering them some part of the money they could save by refraining from unnecessary or over-prolonged treatment. One London hospital offered clinicians the incentive of managing their own budgets at ward level and told them they could spend whatever they saved in other ways. With this incentive to control their own work-load, intensive care, X-rays, to name but one procedure, dropped by 80%.

Despite disgruntlement from many quarters, there are welcome signs that Professor Cochrane is not alone in urging a more scientific look at an often unscientific science in the interests of both better patient care and better value for money. Sir Douglas Black, President of the Royal College of Physicians recently pointed out the dangers to the future of medicine if politicians, administrators and economists took over. 'Audit,' he said, 'is not a threat if it is self-imposed and aims at achieving a measurable improvement in the quality of care through education.' Cochrane himself suggested a future where clinical freedom should be limited by doctors on the evidence of meticulous research.

At present, the medical profession enjoys very considerable freedom in the NHS. Within very wide limits, the doctors can prescribe as they like, and give as many days off as they wish, and decisions about consultation, admission, operation and discharge are in their hands. I imagine that if the research results are implemented there will be considerable limitation of this freedom. Indications for prescriptions, diagnostic tests, admission, length of stay in hospital, etc., will get more and more clearly defined and a sort of 'par for the course' associated with each group of signs and symptoms will be established and those doctors with too many 'strokes' above or below par will be asked to justify themselves before their peers.

If there is hope for this kind of discipline it lies in that phrase 'before their peers'. Cochrane had his doubts. 'No one, I am sure,' he said, 'can visualize the BMA (British Medical Association) with its slogan of "clinical freedom" controlling inflation by controlling the doctors.' How cheered he must have been to read the editorial in the *British Medical Journal* (the journal of the British Medical Association) of 14 April 1978, in which the leader writer tackled the growing problem of medical inflation head on by comparing the British situation with the even more acute health care crisis in America, concluding:

The American dilemma suggests two conclusions relevant to Britain. Firstly, sooner or later all health care systems come up against limitations of finance, for even the United States has to recognize the need to ration scarce resources. Secondly, the medical profession has a special responsibility for helping to find a solution for this problem. If it ducks the challenge, to judge from the experience in the USA, there will be increasing political and administrative pressure designed to regulate its day-to-day activities. The price of professional freedom is clinical self-restraint.

7 Democracy in the Health Service:
The Professionals

Nearly one million people work for the NHS, and between them these people are responsible for spending an annual budget of over £6,000 million, nearly 6% of the Gross National Product. The people in charge of an organization so colossal must be very important and powerful people indeed – if anyone knew who they were.

The crisis of morale from which the employees of the health service are continually suffering is part of a much more profound crisis; a universal crisis of authority. Although doctors still remain the most important decision-makers within the health service, there are less than 80,000 of them in that million, and their power is not what it was. Within living memory the health service was a clearly delimited hierarchical organization where each employee implicitly obeyed his or her professional code, and the order of his or her immediate superiors, and had few doubts or qualms about his or her station in life and position on the health service ladder. Hospitals were run by consultants and a matron and a single hospital secretary, along the inflexible lines of ships or army battalions. The general practitioner was a respected and authoritative figure in the community. A large, respectful and anonymous army of lower orders kept the place clean, filed records, ironed sheets and cooked meals. Everybody knew his or her place and function and kept to it, and that was that.

But all this has changed. Life outside the hospital gates and the GP surgery door has moved on, and if the health service finds itself with a problem of authority and morale on its hands, then it is partly because the social upheavals which affect the world outside have found their way in to its closed and ordered society. The people in the health service are not the people they once were. Old ideas of subservience, of natural respect for authority, a belief in and acknowledgement of hierarchy are becoming outdated, and while certain professions cling to them, notably in medicine and nursing, the rest of the health service employees are profoundly unimpressed. A hospital porter, with the encouragement of his union, now considers he shares an equal claim on society's consideration – and an equal say in the politics of health – with a doctor. An administrator who knows what is good for him no longer issues orders to the people below him. He makes suggestions and negotiates their execution. The health service employees have become politicized and organized. They belong to unions. They make demands. They voice their objections to those ideas with which they disagree. They interfere – according to those who are deeply unhappy with this new state of affairs – with matters which are not their concern. They have adopted practices which have been standard in industry for the last forty years, and applied them to an arena of public life which has always been considered to be outside the political arena. They go slow. They work to rule. They even withdraw their labour despite the traditional sanctity of the patient. And it is becoming more and more evident that those sectors of the health service which have considered themselves above such tactics have been infected by the growing atmosphere of self-preservation. Doctors, in particular, for all their past protests at the selfishness of other unions in the health service, are showing themselves remarkably ready to descend to the market-place and haggle like everyone else.

The democratization of the health service has been hastened, or at least not hindered, by the complete overhaul it received in 1974, when its entire administrative and planning structure was reorganized, disconcerting everybody from the civil servants in the Department of Health to the lowliest hospital clerk. The effects of reorganization are very difficult to convey to anyone who doesn't actually work within the health service. For one thing the very word is so boring, for another the topic is so dry and remote from the intense human interest of the consulting room or the bedside. The average patient is probably quite unaware that anything untoward has gone on. Reorganization has been largely concerned with changing the management structure of the service, with the setting up of committees, the bestowing of new titles, the merging of boards of authority, the introduction of a complicated new system of checks and balances designed to ensure that everyone gets a say. What it is really about is an attempt to introduce modern management and democracy into this vertical and essentially nineteenth-century world, and its effects within the health service have been traumatic. From being a body where decisions were taken automatically by a comparatively small number of people, it has become an organization overwhelmed by the demands of universal consultation. Everyone is now entitled, indeed, obliged, to express an opinion on everything. The structure of authority and decision making is such that everyone *has* to be asked their opinion before any decision can finally be taken. This has paralysed minds and committees and services and produced a crisis of authority from the highest to the lowest.

It is even more unfortunate that these very radical changes in the NHS coincided with a period of economic stringency. The external pressures that made more urgent the need to economize drastically in every area of public expenditure, the plans to cut and to merge services, to close down hospitals and examine the effectiveness of treatments, to make staff redundant, have come at the same time as administrative and political upheavals that have made it very difficult to know where to put the blame. One result of the dust storm of confusion and resentment is that one body of shadowy figures loom larger than they did before – the administrators. If any of the trauma of reorganization has filtered through to the general public it is, through a loud and general casting of blame, and in particular through the focused resentment of unions and doctors alike, that the whole thing is the fault of the administration. Or, in the memorably graphic words of one consultant, that the health service is haemorrhaging into its bureaucracy. Choked by committees, confused by the different layers of authority, it has become so afflicted with self-doubt that it is unable to carry out the simplest action such as the fixing on of a door-hook.

I. Reorganization and the Rise of Bureaucracy

In order to understand some of the alarm and despondency within the health service it is necessary to understand exactly what did take place under reorganization, and how it affects the service the patient receives today. The NHS, since 1974, has been organized into four main tiers of authority. At the top, directly under the current Secretary of State, with a separate Minister responsible for Health, is the civil service Department of Health and Social Security. Its function is largely one of overall planning and budgeting and policy-making, and being directly answerable to Parliament for whatever happens within the health service. The health services for Scotland and Wales and Northern Ireland are run independently under the authority of their separate Secretaries of State. Under the Department in England are fourteen Regional Health Authorities whose function is mainly to facilitate planning and budgeting and to liaise with the Department. Each region is supposed to have certain facilities such as a medical school, regional facilities for particularly specialized and expensive medical procedures such as renal dialysis, and high-security units for dangerous psychiatric patients. Below the Region comes the Area Health Authority, about ninety of them in all, whose main advantage is supposed to be the sharing of administrative boundaries with social services departments. Theoretically this facilitates coordination in those areas where health and social services overlap, such as the care of old people or the mentally ill. There is great argument about which is the superfluous administrative tier in the new structure since most people feel that there are too many, but both the Region and the Area can prove their lineage from some previous decision-making body. Regional Authorities largely replaced the old Regional Hospital Boards, and the Area Health Authority, the tier which draws the most animosity, replaced a motley collection of different hospital boards and executive councils.

Below the Area is the District Health Authority. About two

hundred of these are responsible for the day-to-day work of the NHS in its contact with patients. Some services are organized on a regional, some on an Area and some on a District basis, but for the most part the general public will be more aware of the District if it is aware of administrative complexities at all. Most people tend to think of the health service strictly in terms of their own doctor or their local hospital. The luxury of thinking so small is not given to the one million employees of the health service. What they have become aware of, more than of the new tiers of authority, is the proliferation of committees and consultative procedures. Nobody, it seems, can make a simple decision without informing twenty other people, or attending six different committees, or obtaining the consensus of at least a dozen statutory bodies. If anybody has an idea it may take two years to put into practice by the time it has risen up the levels of decision-making and sunk back down again.

The NHS wasn't organized this way out of simple perversity, however much its individual employees would like to think so. There is a hard streak of common sense and necessity in the new planning apparatus, and in the admittedly over-cautious system of checks and balances that have been introduced. In the past, large chunks of money have been distributed according to the individual and local pressure. The overall view has now officially been introduced. The idea is that somebody at some stage should be balancing the claimant voices and competing needs and making rational decisions that take into account the needs of the community for all kinds of health care. It may be all very well for a consultant to claim a new operating theatre because the old one is badly lit, ill-equipped, out of date and unsatisfactory in every way, but there may be acute pressure in the same district for a new children's ward, an old people's day centre, a maternity wing. The necessity of balancing the evidence and making these decisions, difficult and depressing as they are, is the province of the new bureaucracy and goes a long way towards explaining why the medical profession is so extremely antagonistic to the powers of the new administration. The new emphasis is on consensus management, balanced by the consumer voice as represented by two hundred Community Health Councils. The different professional voices can be heard on a multiplicity of committees. It is no wonder if more and more groups within the health service have despaired of getting their voice heard through the somnolent murmur of so many committees, and have resorted to more militant methods.

Presumably to their subsequent regret, the medical profession in particular originally wanted to play more part in the administration of the service. They may have found, like other groups before them, that too much democracy may be altogether too much of a good thing. Administrators in the past were people who were there to see that the medical profession got everything it wanted. Doctors must be wishing it were still so, as they grow to see administrators as people put there by a malign providence to frustrate their every desire.

'Nowadays,' says one, 'the magic of the physician is being breached, the whole thing is being challenged. Consultants have been bashed on three things – they feel they've borne the brunt of wage restraint, then there's the government seeking to withdraw pay-beds, then there's reorganization, the way in which they feel they've lost a degree of influence in the hospitals. Doctors had much more sway in the past and now we're paying the price for doctor power. Change has to be at the expense of those who've had more than their fair share of influence and doctors are no longer the big fish. In the hospital service everyone else has always been there to enable the consultant, the prima donna, to do his job. Now, for the first time, someone else is actually preventing the doctor from doing his job.'

And yet the irony is that patients go to hospitals to see doctors, not the cleaner or the shop-steward or the administrator. The loss of self-image and self-respect, the bewilderment of the authority figure whose authority is no longer taken for granted is vividly expressed by the evidence of the Royal College of Surgeons to the Royal Commission. With more than a streak of self-pity the Royal College complains that the patients' needs:

seem to have become subordinate to the political needs of legislators, the cold calculations of planners, the officious inflexibility of
administrators and the thrusting self-interest of NHS staff of all
kinds ... Bewilderment at the proliferation of bureaucracy, with its
attendant paraphernalia of offices, committees and non-productive
staff. The profession feels itself to be drowning in a sea of paper and
deafened by waves of verbiage, and it finds its own informed statements on how patients should be cared for largely unheard in a
tumult of other voices, a consciousness of resentment amounting
almost to hostility towards the profession itself, exhibited increasingly by politicians, the media and other groups of workers within
the service.

If asked, both the doctor and the administrator (and every
other worker in the health service) would say in all sincerity that
they had the patients' interests at heart. But they have quite
different ways of interpreting those interests, and they may be
considering the problem in the light of quite different facts.
One, with the threat of a limited budget, already over-stretched,
has to decide what will most benefit the most patients within the
limitations set by finite resources. The other has a sense of overwhelming local need, possibly prompted by his own particular
hobby-horse, certainly prompted by ways in which he genuinely
thinks he personally could give a better service to his own particular patients. The restrictions of bureaucracy seem to him
to be cold-blooded and petty. The demands of the consultant
seem, to the administrators, to be narrow-minded and auto-
cratic. These conflicts show up in the very machinery that is
meant to bring them together in a grand reconciliation. One of
the aims of reorganization was to bring about consensus of all
the groups within the health service, but on its present showing
the service seems to defy consensus like a body rejecting a transplant. The grass-roots committee which best shows the intentions of the new system is the District Management Team. The
District Management Team is supposed to be responsible for
both day-to-day decisions and policy on the District level, and it
is composed of six regular members – the District Administrator, the District Physician, the District Finance Officer, the

District Nursing Officer, a representative consultant and a representative GP. Its aim is consensus of different interests and many people claim that it works very well, that it is a valuable innovation. But where it fails it shows up the deep rifts between the professional groups, and the equally deep rifts between members of the same profession where their interests are shown to conflict. Doctors, in particular, are not a homogenous group, and experience is showing that a doctor on a committee often feels quite unable to commit his colleagues to any course of action simply because he might agree with it personally. The only factor that unites one doctor with another is a shared distrust of administrators, with whom they will sometimes classify their colleagues in community medicine.

Management by consensus has been called a system of management designed to ensure that no one is managed, and the responsibility of making shared decisions and the consciousness of representing conflicting interests reduces some DMTs (District Management Teams) to helpless inactivity. The only decisions they feel capable of making are the simple ones – decisions which an administrator could have made in the past with eyes closed. If this issue is something big they can split altogether. The consultant resigned from one DMT over the issue of removing pay-beds from local hospitals, and both doctors resigned over the issue of changing a maternity ward into a geriatric unit.

'The two medical representatives belong to their peers,' said a fellow DMT member, 'and the other four hang together. The original theory was that this team could produce a consensus, but it can't. The GP may agree on the need for the elderly but if it impinges on his peer group he'll back out. Basically a committee is just there to obstruct, to slow the whole process down.'

One paradoxical result of all this consultation and democracy is that the determined and manipulative can still get what they want simply by turning the lack of authority to their own advantage. The management consultancy firm of McKinsey's, who produced the original plans on which the reorganized health service was based, climbed down somewhat when individual members of the firm presented their evidence to the Royal Commission on the National Health Service.[1] 'At a recent meeting,' they wrote, 'none of the area administrators in one region were able to point out a single case where patients had benefited from reorganization.' They added that the NHS, far from being a homogenous body united by singleness of purpose was 'an uneasy coalition of thirty or more proudly independent and mutually suspicious professions'. Certainly other evidence presented to the Royal Commission illustrated vividly the conflicting interests within the health service. Hundreds of separate organizations presented their ideas on how the whole thing should and could be run, and hardly one of them agreed with another. How, then, can they be expected to agree on a single committee? Without a clear line of authority the health service will continue to inch itself forward against the counter-pressure of competing vested interests. Only now the whole business is slower than it was. A nursing officer is quoted in a report on the reorganized service to have said:

What is generally complained about is the abundance of meetings. Every day you are at a meeting and what is also complained about is that from these meetings come no decisions. I think this is because there are so many committees that have to be consulted before any decision can be made. It's got to go to the Community Health Council, the Local Medical Committee, the District Management Team, the Nurses' Advisory Committee.[2]

And the process is very slow indeed. Even assuming a decision emerges at the end of it, the whole process can have taken months, even years. 'In administration nobody knows what they can and they can't do,' complained a hospital administrator. 'It took me three months to spend some money by which time the costs had gone up by £50.' His area administrator pointed out the impossibility of getting a decision quickly, given the consultation procedure. 'If you're asked for a view,' he said, 'you have to go to five professional advisory bodies who might meet only every three months. Say we're asked for a view on a policy matter like abortion or pay-beds, we're then talking about at least three or four months. It's simply nonsense to ask for a decision on something in three weeks. People at the top just don't realize the problems.'

At its most basic, literally nuts and bolts level, the new processes can mean similar delays in the most practical and everyday problems. The case often quoted is of the orthopaedic consultants in Hull who ran out of the particular size of screw they needed for bones.

It is now much more difficult to get things. There have been delays in requisitions. Six months ago we ordered screws for bones. When we ran out of the old stock I was told that the order had not arrived despite a number of requests, so we have to use five-eighths screws. I contacted the supplies department directly but nothing happened, and eventually the senior orthopaedist contacted the district administrator and sorted it out. We found that there were no less than eleven channels for requisition. This does not help us.[3]

So who are the faceless people who, alone it seems, have gained such power from reorganization, who withhold screws from orthopaedic surgeons and thousands of pounds from deserving causes in every corner of the health service while they, some say darkly, live off the fat of the land? Their menace seems to be larger than their actual numbers. Out of 914,068 employees of the NHS – excluding the independents like general practitioners and dentists – 105,781 can be classified as administrative and clerical staff, and the largest group of these is composed of clerical and secretarial staff. Actual administrators, by name, only add up to 17,300 individuals. The largest single professional group in the health service is actually formed by the 405,817 nurses, and nobody ever complains that there are too many of them. Administrators are more remarkable for their growth rate than for their actual presence. In the year between 1971 and 1974 they nearly doubled themselves, and the system is self-generating. The more committees and decisions that are involved, the more administrators are required to keep the system going if it goes at all. Whatever else they do, administrators, the butt of the medical profession and media alike, have a talent for facelessness even when some particularly inept piece of public relations results in a routine display of administrator-bashing.

What do we mean by an administrator? Does the term include pay clerks and typists and medical record keepers and catering officers? The health service's own statistics throw in storekeeper-clerks and farm managers, along with machine operators and Prescription Pricing Authority staff. If one divided the health service and administration into those whose function it is directly to look after patients, and those whose job it is to look after the health service, maybe the figures become less alarming. In every country, as governments struggle to exercise some control over the runaway rise in health expenditure, the costs of administration are rising steeply. The greater the involvement of the state the greater the increase in the number of officials and bureaucrats. The creation of new departments such as planning and national financing means the creation of large bureaucracies to look after them, but it is a point well worth making that piecemeal systems involving private health care and independent insurance companies have far heavier administrative costs than the NHS which is financed from general taxation. The British United Provident Association estimates its administrative and development costs at 12%, much higher than the National Health Service's $3\frac{1}{2}\%$.

Administrators and their subordinate staff are there theoretically to relieve medical and nursing staff of duties which take them from their patients, to manage the system, to provide personnel services, to organize the supplies, to pay everybody else, to look after buildings and manage the money. There are other groups of administrators as well, other than purely bureaucratic ones. The nursing and medical professions have shown a tendency to want their own internal administration as part of a career structure, though one large area health authority conducted a survey into the number of nursing administrators among its nursing staff and found that administration hadn't swamped the nursing service to the extent that was feared. Out of 10,000 nurses in the area, only 0·5% were actually involved in administration that removed them completely from the patients. The rest were carrying out patient care.

The ratio of administrators to patients in the NHS is currently estimated to be one per 5·6 occupied hospital beds, although if one remembers that only 10% of patient care actually involves hospital beds this figure is not quite as alarming as it sounds. Modern administration is carried out by very different sorts of people from the old-style hospital secretary. For a start, it is surprising how many people in health service administration are university graduates who have undergone specific training after leaving university. The traditional administrator, like those people who govern schools and charities, was a professional committee man, often a retired member of the armed forces, or it might be somebody who had come into the service as a clerk and worked his or her way up the civil service career ladder. Today, apart from the younger breed of graduate-administrator there are also more people who have had their management experience in fields other than health, and contribute to the breakdown of the isolation of health care from the rest of the working world. Young administrators have a different, perhaps a more positive idea of their function than the administrator of the past.

'When you talk to health service managers,' said one, 'you can get a very narrow view. It's a considerable barrier to imaginative thinking in the health service. But it is getting better. Administrators can have quite a lot of good informal pressure. By keeping abreast of what goes on in health care an administrator can be aware of changes. If you can demonstrate your ideas properly consultants will take notice. For example, there might be a way of streamlining the use of operating theatres. Administration has become more sophisticated in the last fifteen years. Before, a doctor and a nurse could do everything between them. The administrator's role is now the production of substantive evidence. His expertise in the past was in support of services but he can help clinical and nursing services develop to a high standard.'

Outside a hospital, the most important function of a good administrator is to provide an informed and broadly based view, a liaison, both within the health service, and between the health service and the outside world. The advantage of a thorough planning procedure staffed by well-informed administrators is that it can hold up bad or inequitable decisions that might otherwise go through on a nod or a wink. The disadvantage of the new procedure is that it is equally efficient at holding up perfectly good decisions, even decisions that by their very nature ought to be made with some speed. Take a simple example, a request for funds for a children's playground in a mental handicap hospital. The member of staff who originally has this idea, who works out how much it will cost, what staffing it will take, what piece of ground can be provided for it, has first to convince his or her colleagues within the particular institution that the idea is a good and practical one. Then it enters the labyrinth of the bureaucracy. It passes to the Medical Executive Committee, where the representative for mental handicap has to put it forward as a good and practical idea to colleagues from other specialities like paediatrics or ear, nose and throat, who have also come with what they think are very good and practical ideas for ways in which money could be spent. Assuming it passes the Medical Executive Committee, it then goes on to the District Management Team who have to balance it out against claims for resources from primary care teams in the district, from the different hospital departments, from a dozen different specialities. Once past the DMT the idea goes up to the Area and is put to the Area Management Team which will be considering claims from anything between two and five different Districts. Somehow the quality of the original idea, the drive of an individual doctor, the efficiency of an individual administrator have all become as nothing in this tangle of procedure. The system has taken over, and it takes its time.

'This can all take anything from six months to two years,' says the man with the idea, in pardonable frustration. 'On these joint committees I suppose there might be one or two people who actually touch patients in need. They want to know if there will be any revenue consequences. The problem now is that it is all balance and no movement. There's total inertia – and tell me, where has my voice gone by then?'

II. The Voice of the Unions

If the voice of the individual professional in the health service has been muffled by reorganization and by the constant shuffling of bureaucratic papers, certain other voices in the health service are clamouring more loudly and more urgently than ever before. They do not necessarily represent the interest of individual groups of patients but they certainly represent the interests of individual groups of workers. One of the most urgent, and intractable, problems facing the health service today is the conflict between its dual role as provider of health care to the population, and as the country's largest employer. For thousands of people in the health service democracy has not gone far enough, and in the form in which it has been introduced is too bound by bureaucracy to be effective. The new voice comes from the encroachment on an isolated and traditional service by the rough and tumble of the industrial world outside. The professional associations which have hitherto held power within health services, in particular the medical associations, are being threatened by the rise of other groups within the service. As David Owen wrote when he was Minister of Health:

There has been a sizeable shift in the balance of power, reflecting a shift going on in the country as a whole. Nurses now have a voice to be reckoned with and so do the health service unions. No Minister of Health, whether Tory or Labour, can ever again handle the health service simply by squaring things with the BMA. There are other forces now and they are here for keeps.[4]

1974 was accounted by many to be the most turbulent year in the history of the NHS. Nurses went on strike for the first time. So did almost every other class of health worker, from X-ray technicians to junior doctors. The rash of disputes reminded the general public that their health service was dependent on the work of an enormous army of labourers who, like galley slaves, were sick of being the unseen power that moved the ship along, and had flung off their shackles for a turn on the decks. And they weren't simply coming up for air. At a time when reorganization was shifting the power balances within the service, individual groups wanted to make sure that their voice was heard. A political adviser within the Department who was closely involved at the time pointed out that the issues behind the disputes lay much deeper than protest against the pay policy.

Reorganization caused considerable disruption and it gave the unions the opportunity to think hard about the structure. It all coincided with the coming of age of COHSE (Confederation of Health Service Employees) as a competitor with NUPE (National Union of Public Employees). In every sector there are competing unions – NUPE, TGWU (Transport and General Workers' Union), and COHSE among the manual workers, and among the nurses there have been battles between The Royal College of Nursing and COHSE which represents the psychiatric nurses. Then there are unions competing for the hospital doctors. There was a desire within COHSE to show strength, to atone for having gone along with the Industrial Relations Bill. It is an inherent part of the complexity of the operation that any one group can disrupt all the rest. All the groups now realize their power and conflicts between groups are exacerbated by this plethora of trade unions – there is no clear demarcation anywhere. What's more, the management structure is too complicated and all negotiations involve a process by consensus. Basically, it all depends on muscle.

So, flexing their muscles is what the health service unions have been doing ever since, over every kind of health issue from the political struggles over private medicine in public hospitals to their own pay, to heating in the hospital kitchen, laundry facilities and job demarcation. The press and public together have found the manifestations of industrial battle within a supposedly caring service very shocking. They are shocked when non-medical unions like COHSE and NUPE go on strike over issues like hours of work and back-pay when patients can be seen to suffer as a result. They are equally shocked when the same unions go on strike over political issues such as the abolition of private medicine from within the National Health Service. They are shocked when patients have to eat cold breakfasts or sleep in unwashed sheets, or even be sent home because industrial action has closed down some area of the service. For the first time, workers in the health service have dared to stand up and demonstrate that there are areas and issues where the short-term needs of the individual patient no longer come first. The shock of the groups in the health service who did not at first press their own claims at the cupidity and self-interest of the rest was also tinged with resentment at the thought that they might get away with it. Even the doctors have caught up now and show a remarkable readiness to ditch their training and their principles and join in the kind of undignified free-for-all they condemn. The atmosphere of dispute is a very contagious one, and when the basic unity of a service has been undermined and a common sense of purpose lost, then group self-interest rises to the surface with surprising ease.

There are over forty different associations representing the working forces in the health service from the British Medical Association to the Transport and General Workers' Union. They don't all like to think of themselves as trade unions but as more of them relinquish their aloof professional status to fight for their rights in the same arena, trade unions is what they become. While the health service is the biggest employer in the country, it has been far from the most generous. The economic pressures and privations which are interfering with the execution of its duties are also interfering with the private lives of its employees. Where the end of a service is seen to be noble, there is often exploitation involved, and health workers have for too long been tending the rest of us at their own expense. There is no logical reason why nurses or technicians or laundry workers should be denied a reasonable wage just because they do good. What has happened within the health service over the last few years is that the people who work farthest away from the patient were the first to feel free to press claims with any degree of force, because they were the most free from the emotional restraints and responsibilities felt by other workers, in particular the nurses. It may or may not be an indictment on modern society, but in very few corners of it are people prepared any longer to sacrifice themselves and their families for the sake of health or any other public good. Inevitably, union members put their own and their families' interests before the interests of the health service at large. Only in the more politicized, urban areas such as the East End of London, where the NHS is the biggest employer, does job protection become inextricably mixed up with politics, in particular with opposition to health service cuts, as a local official explained:

As far as the unions are concerned, the problems are complex. They feel that to accept cuts is to opt out of changing the structure of society, they feel they need to change the awareness of people. It is very difficult for them to have a positive role in the health service but their influence to obstruct is very great. In the present system there is not much to promote and they don't want to be part of the present system. The social implications of health service cuts for the East End are very serious. The unions do their homework. The health service is a very big employer and union strength is in numbers. Membership has increased from 25% to 60% in ten years. The health service is a naïve organization. It has been possible for the unions to gain territory and reorganization has allowed a great deal of territorial gain. Shop-stewards are querying every replacement and time off for union activities has built up.

Nevertheless, the issues that fire the unions most, to the extent of leading to industrial action, for the most part concern their own pay and jobs. The London Hospital was closed to admissions because ancillary workers took industrial action in pursuit of back-pay. Local spending cuts caused a strike in Liverpool hospitals. Overtime rotas put Surrey hospitals under siege. Fears over union redundancies, proposals to close hospitals with further loss of jobs, parking facilities, all these have caused trouble in hospitals over the past year. With 70% of the health service budget going on manpower, and with administrators constantly looking for ways to cut back, the unions will be kept busy protecting their jobs for some time yet.

However, self-interest is not the only motive at issue. There is a great deal of concern over the power structure within the NHS and a basic feeling among workers that they must have a voice in the running of their own organization. The Transport and General Workers' Union stated clearly in its evidence to the Royal Commission that their expectation of involvement in decision-making in the health service was simply an extension of their universal belief in industrial democracy. As the health service is the biggest employer in the country then there is all the more reason for all its workers to want to be involved in its running. Since the rise of the bureaucracy it could be argued that the equal rise of industrial democracy provides a useful counter-balance to administrator-power. Unions may feature as villains acting in their own interests, but they are also quick to act in what they see as the defence of the service, in the protection of patients against sweeping closures or unfeeling bureaucrats.

There is a new element too, the rise of professionalism in groups ancillary to medicine. Where techniques become more specialized or responsibility has been devolved, other workers are demanding independence and recognition of their value. The growing intransigence of these workers comes as a result of responsibility already given but not recognized by adequate status or financial reward. One obvious case is that of the nurses in the long-stay areas who do a heavy percentage of very responsible work because of the absence of the medical profession. Contributors to a discussion reported in the *British Medical Journal* on this very problem – the devolution of responsibility in the health service – pointed out that 'if the nurses do 99% of the work in the chronic, long-stay sector, providing the care, determining the environment, then shouldn't they be formally allowed responsibility?'[5] The focus of this particular discussion was the way in which doctors were losing power to other workers, and the way in which these other workers were no longer prepared even to accept the automatic leadership of the doctor in a health care team. What the participants of the discussion saw, ominously inserted in their door, was the thin end of the wedge. 'As doctors,' said one, Dr Antony Clare,

we may welcome the growth of a group of people with an expertise and a wish for responsibility . . . but what if they're the carriers of an alien philosophy? For instance, does the new control over radiology departments mean that there are going to be time and motion studies, clocking in and out, problems about night cover – a whole new way of looking at things? Consultants have no great objection to the technician developing his expertise, indeed, taking over aspects of management. What worries them is that the new professionals will take control, use it quite differently and base it on a quite alien philosophy to that underlying clinical medicine.

And here is the essence of the problem underlying democracy in the health service, not that more and more groups have power without responsibility, but that they see their responsibilities differently. There is a trade union philosophy, a management philosophy, a medical philosophy, but no health service philosophy. The case is not hopeless, although it sometimes seems to present horrible difficulties. For a start, the level of concern about the health service is high among all groups of workers. In their evidence to the Royal Commission the main health service unions presented themselves as the champions of the original ideals of the health service, defending its social purpose against the attacks of doctors, politicians and administrators alike. The challenge facing the health service is to channel this desire for participation so that it works for the benefit of patients and public alike rather than leading to a situation of stalemate. The Welsh Office produced a paper recommending the introduction of ancillary health workers and union representatives on to Area Health Authorities, and absorption of all the voices in the health service into the existing machinery.[6] This may be one answer – if only to ensure that the more aggressive voices in the health service become bogged down in the same mass of committees that have absorbed everyone else. But this does not tackle the heart of the matter – the lack of unity among health service workers. There remains a hard job of public relations work to be done within the health service itself. An outstanding Secretary of State could restore some of the original idealism to the health service, but even under a Labour government the prospect required a great deal of optimism. Under a Tory administration dedicated both to radical public spending cuts and to bolstering the private sector, belief in the ideals of the National Health Service is likely to suffer still more. In the meantime all the workers in the service, from doctors to tea-ladies, could benefit from some basic information and education – perhaps drawn up by specialists in community medicine – as to what the health service is for, how it is run and what it can achieve provided its workers regain their sense of purpose.

8 Democracy in the Health Service: The Amateurs

It is a strange fact that although everyone knows the health service is in a state of crisis, although the health service is universally famous as a symbol of hopeless collapse, nevertheless, most of its patients continue to think it is wonderful. A particularly gloomy television programme about the demise of medicine as we know it panned its cameras through a large and overcrowded hospital waiting room and asked its occupants what they thought about it all. Everyone questioned was perversely and unreasonably happy with the treatment and the attention they received. Ah yes, said the consultants interviewed later – the patients don't know the difference between good and bad medicine and we do, which is why we are unhappy and they aren't. None the less, research shows that most users of health services are generally satisfied with what they get. Which is as well, because in many ways, the health service is as much shaped by the demands and expectations of the general public as it is by the more obvious controls exercised by the professionals.

Public interest in, and pressure on, the health service cannot be expected to be a minutely informed and rational influence. One of the problems facing anyone who wishes to use the force of public opinion in changing the health service is that when the public are patients they are incapacitated from too much action and when they are not, they can't identify with those who are. If acute medicine and emergency procedures predominate in the public imagination it is because public interest in health is based on emotional identification, and individual and family experience. Public interest cannot be expected to rest on a broad base, but it can channel itself very effectively and deeply into individual causes dear to the individual heart, such as maternity services or handicapped children. The innumerable pressure groups that are set up, based on different diseases and conditions, owe their strength to the fact that they are run by people whose families have that particular problem, or who have been through that particular ordeal. This is one reason why the Community Health Councils, which were set up to channel the public view, tend to be dominated by the strongly motivated members of special interest groups, rather than reflect a rational and objective interest in the service as a whole.

As a result the health service reflects the short-term view taken by most of the people who use it. The health service reflects the attitudes of the society from which it springs and, because it is directly concerned with caring for people, it reflects the values we place, not only on human life but on the quality of that life. There are five main ways in which our attitudes reach the health service and consequently shape it. One is by the sometimes unconscious expectations we have of it, and the demands which we subsequently make. The corollary to this is our reaction to medical advice and treatment which, despite our anxiety to get it in the first place, we often fail to follow. Secondly, there is the image of the service as we see it and follow it through the media, the fathomless wells of interest we show in some aspects of it, and the equally bottomless pits of apathy we reserve for others. Thirdly, we can participate directly in its workings as individuals. If we ask a question instead of being passively examined, if we demand an explanation instead of allowing ourselves to be patted on the head, then we are personally doing our bit towards making the health service more open-minded and responsive to our needs. Fourthly, as groups, through voluntary agencies and Friends of Hospitals we can press our own special interest and polish up our corner. And finally, as members of Community Health Councils and Patients' Committees, or as members of the audience at Community Health Councils meetings we have the opportunity to become actively involved in the problems of the service in our particular district.

Expectation in the health service is a continually changing element with only one constant factor. It grows. 'Everything in the health service has changed for the better,' said a health worker who had been involved in the service for more than forty years. 'But the thing that has changed most of all is public demand. It's a progression you can't stop. In the 1930s if you had appendicitis you thought you were going to die; the same with renal failure. These days everyone expects a transplant. In the 1930s, if you were in a car accident it was too bad. Now you expect marvellous treatment. We should say "If these are the re-sources which the community can provide then this is the level to which we can provide the service." We should get the public to decide how much health service they're going to get for their money. There should be some way of relating needs to commit-ment to pay. People understand that not everyone can own a Rolls-Royce but they don't apply the same principle to health care.'

Every element in contact with the health service, the people who work in it, the press, the public, expect more and more and become more and more dissatisfied when they don't get it. Over thirty years of a National Health Service which has promised the best of health care available to anyone who needs it has blurred our sense of perspective on the problems. We think we are getting worse and worse off, when we are simply expecting more and more. One of the gulfs that exists between patients and health service workers is a misunderstanding over what one side offers and what the other side wants. To many people the main value of a doctor, or of a health service, is not so much that he cures specific conditions on a scientific basis, but that he makes people feel better. Making people feel better is a very different and a much more vague proposition from curing them. It involves human contact and faith on both sides. This role for medicine stems directly from the priest and the witch-doctor and it exists hand in hand with the whole body scanners and the men in white coats. Calling in a doctor is as much a propitiatory action as sacrificing a goat. No priest ever examined entrails with more display of concentration and inarticulate authority than the average doctor saying, 'Aha' over an expectant patient. Modern society takes a conscious stand against death, the reaper, and the doctor is the intermediary. The health service has been allowed to appropriate the great events of life to itself so that very few people in industrial Western society see people born or see people die. These processes have become medical conditions to be tended in scientific fashion by men in masks. The comings and goings of life have been transferred from the heart of the community to an antiseptic medical airport lounge.

The health professionals, struggling with the confusion of roles projected on them by the public, feel with some resentment that they are being called upon to do work for which they weren't trained. The public at large sees a doctor as a paternal caring figure. As a result the G P who partly considers himself to have been trained as a technician is faced with every complexity of social and psychological stress. With the breakdown of support within the community, with the increasing isolation of people in industrialized urban communities, with the breakdown of the Church as a source of spiritual comfort and certainty and practical help, the G P has become a central point for all those seeking help. And it is often help which he feels unable or unwilling to give. Doctors faced with patients have a job of diagnostic detective-work to do and they can be confused, even a little put out, at the way patients are beginning to intrude themselves and their personal problems into the clinical arena. Those general practitioners who may once have had ambitions to continue in hospital medicine find themselves cast in a role of confessor for which they may feel totally unfit.

'I'm a great ear,' said one bitterly. 'I'll listen to anything. Family problems, failing marriages – they come and tell me everything, but that's not what I was trained for. I'm a scientist. My job is to treat disease.'

Paradoxically, while the NHS groans under the pressure of demand for advice which it doesn't always feel fit to give, the potential of the general public for demanding actual curative medicine has hardly been tapped yet. Such surveys as have been carried out into the health and attitude to health of the population show rather startlingly that, although we do little about it, most of us think we are sick. A number of surveys have been carried out in recent years which prove that feeling unwell is normal. Hard-working doctors may be personally convinced that the public exists simply to besiege them with a wealth of trivialities but under the circumstances it looks as though the public shows remarkable restraint. In a survey carried out in Southwark it was found that 52% of those screened needed further investigation or treatment. In the fourteen days prior to the interview only a very small proportion of those complaining of symptoms had been to see a doctor, and for every individual taking a prescribed medicine two more were taking medicines they had bought over the counter. In another survey in Bermondsey in 1971 95% of the people taking part had felt ill during the previous fortnight though only a tiny percentage of them had presented themselves to a doctor.[1] It seems that feeling below par in one way or another is so common that most of us grin and bear it. Another survey, conducted by Dunnell and Cartwright,[2] found 90% of its interviewees with definable symptoms over a two-week period and in the Rochester survey in New York, where families were asked to keep a twenty-eight-day health diary they recorded at least one complaint on 21·8% of all days.[3] On 93·2% of these days they simply treated themselves. Maybe if asked specifically to record how you feel rather than reply to the normal polite social inquiry, most people will think of something rather than disappoint the interviewer.

Nevertheless, despite this restraint, and despite the fact that most of us are fitter and healthier than we have ever been before, the number of consultations and inquiries set in motion is going up and up. The number of referrals to out patients rose by 30% between 1950 and 1970. The annual number of hospital admissions doubled in the same period. But despite all this contact with the service one of the most interesting aspects of the public's attitude to medical care is that a very large, and consequently expensive and wasteful number of us go away and ignore whatever advice or treatment we may have been given. The public as taxpayers have every right to be annoyed with the public as patients for such a wasteful attitude to health care.

Different studies show that up to 50% of patients forget what the doctor has told them within five minutes of seeing him. Why do they go then? Is it because simple human contact and re-assurance is more important than actual treatment? Or is it simply to allay evil spirits by visiting the oracle. It seems that improvement of these figures is partly in the doctors' hands. The more effort doctors put into explaining the treatment, the more likely it is to be followed. An American study also showed that doctors gave the least information to their worst informed patients, thus continuing a cycle of ignorance and apathy and poor communication.

Although most people claim some interest in their own health, the level of knowledge about health in the community is relatively low. One study shows that 54% of people don't know where their kidneys are, 50% couldn't find their stomach and 40% had no idea where the bladder was. Even the members of Community Health Councils, who might be supposed to have a deeper interest in the subject than most of us, have been shown to have read very little about health services beyond the booklet produced specially for them. What most people learn about health services and medicine in general comes to them through the media of newspapers, magazines and television – sources of information which by their very nature are not noted for the measured, reflective approach to any subject they tackle. In the field of health where there is no shortage of vividly dramatic, harrowing or emotional material, it is not surprising if the con-centration is almost entirely on the sensational or the frivolous. It is rare to find reporting that is allowed the space to explain the issues behind the running of a health service, or the pro-vision of a treatment, or the history behind a dispute. New developments in medicine are often reported uncritically, par-ticularly where they might offer the bone of a miraculous cure. Hospitals are featured if they are either temples to the tech-nological marvel or rat-infested Victorian workhouses that offer all the ingredients of a rich scandal. If patients have died, or look likely to die, as a result of bad food or plumbing or an industrial dispute, that makes the best copy of all.

A study of coverage given to health by the national press in a random week indicates the level of seriousness with which health news is treated by newspapers. In the week beginning 22 August 1977, the Health Education Council issued its annual report, but the general apathy which greets attempts at preventive health or health education was well reflected in the coverage it received. The *Daily Express*, *Daily Mirror* and *Daily Telegraph* ignored it completely. Different levels of seriousness exist side by side in the same paper as illustrated in the *Daily Mirror* which carried one frivolous headline, IT'S A WINNER, SAY WIVES ON THE TRIKE (tricyclic pill), and yet three days later published a very sensible and informative piece by Marjorie Proops on the contraceptive pill. Women's pages and magazines have shown an increasingly responsible and informative attitude to health matters, and can be counted on more and more for well-informed coverage of medical developments that might interest their readers. This encouragement to women to take an interest in the control of their own bodies has been one of the side-effects of women's liberation and it has had a marked effect on certain parts of the health service such as obstetrics, family planning and abortion. It shows very vividly what can be accomplished when the public takes the trouble to inform itself on medical matters, and on its own health need, and then speaks up.

The changes that have taken place in obstetrics in the last ten years are the best illustration of what can happen when a concerned public and a concerned press get together to bring about change. Many women, together with the organizations that concern themselves specifically with maternity services and childbirth, were increasingly concerned at the overkill of medical technology which they felt was affecting the normal process of childbirth, both in hospital and at home. Questioning by these organizations, by women themselves, and a great deal of coverage in the national press and on television on the subject of childbirth has slowed the process down and made many obstetric units more responsive to the needs of their patients. The fact that nearly all obstetric patients are in good health, and that many of them question the treatment they receive, has made this a particularly receptive branch of the health service, and there is no doubt that the continuing debate on obstetric practices conducted in the media has helped to keep obstetricians and midwives on their toes.

Where there is scope for great concern there is also scope for an equal amount of irresponsibility and, unhappily, a great deal of media coverage of medical matters is irresponsible. On the same day one of the popular dailies covered two medical stories connected with child health. One, which filled a page, was devoted to the struggles of a young mother whose child had a rare disease for which treatment was hard to find. The story was written very emotionally and it made a strong plea for the very large sums of money needed to treat the child and its fellow sufferers, without pointing out that the money must come necessarily from some other, equally under-funded area of the health service or from extra taxation. In the same edition of the same paper, in a low corner of a page, without benefit of headline or photograph, a short paragraph gave the astonishing information that thousands of children each year were born brain-damaged because their mothers had smoked during pregnancy. There is no doubt which issue is the most important to the community, which condition affects the most people or which might be most tractable to action, but the one offered a strong human story and the other did not. From the journalistic point of view one was simply better copy than the other.

One other important point was involved; the burden of responsibility. It is much more palatable for a newspaper to thump some mythical table and say 'the government must do this', than for it to thump the same table and tell its readers to do something. Readers don't like being moralized at, although they are very sympathetic to stories which attack some distant but culpable authority. A story about health could almost be said to be interesting to readers in inverse proportion to the responsibility it puts on them. Stories with what one might call a cosmetic bias are one exception to this rule. There has been an enormous increase over the years in knowledgeable coverage of diet and exercise and self-maintenance, particularly in women's magazines, although national newspapers like the *Sunday Times* have joined in. Women in the past have been more responsive to the idea of self-improvement than men, but the widespread habits of dieting and jogging and health maintenance are catching on. How far reading about health maintenance is a substitute for doing anything about it no one has yet discovered.

If following newspaper diets is one way we can affect our own health, there are also direct ways in which we can affect the health service. In the past such action has mainly been concerned with fund-raising for individual causes by a plethora of voluntary groups such as Action for the Crippled Child, MenCap and Help the Aged. The value of groups like these, both in raising hard cash and in bringing about change in their particular quarter of the health service, is enormous, but they do little to rearrange the service as a whole, nor is this their function. What they are there for is to improve their bit of it, and in this way they act in much the same manner as the individual consultant who is competing with other individual consultants for one slice of the cake. Because public interest in the health service depends so strongly on individual experience and empathy it seems likely that groups like these will continue to catch the public imagination more than Community Health Councils with their broad spectrum of interest, although Community Health Councils have the advantage of reflecting local needs and feelings.

If the public can identify with a particular group or medical condition, they also become very heated over threats to the local service. You could call this kind of participation in the health service 'reactive participation'. They are not planning for the future or taking a measured view, but reacting hotly to whatever they see as a threat. The reactive view, together with the voluntary group, has been the main channel of interest in the health service up till now. At every level of the health service, staff find that the public become very heated over any visible threat to the delivery of acute medicine. In one area of south-east England where years of promise to rebuild the district hospitals have disintegrated with the falling pound, the administrator reflected on the impossibility of marrying public expectation with government funds and national plans. 'There is public pressure for acute services,' he explained. 'We are only meant to have one district general hospital in each health district – this is national policy, but we have problems with local expectations. The people want a local hospital in each town. It is much easier to stimulate public support for acute hospitals than anything else. It is more dramatic, it is more interesting, it's something that affects them all, they relate to it. There is a fever heat about the health service in the South East, an almost obsessional interest. People just don't have the same attitudes in the North, or the same expectations.'

A regional official, talking about the same problem, reflected wryly that the general public wasn't noted for its interest in the long-term. 'They're not interested in statistical proof of things which are likely to happen to them in thirty years' time. They're not interested in mental health although one in seven will end up in a psychiatric hospital. They're not interested in geriatric services – in fact anything in the future they're not interested in. Things in the health service get done in response to clamour from outside and the public response is largely for life and death things. In H—— they want a new hospital but we can't afford to build one any more so the people are outraged. You could say that "thousands marched". We have a health service that reflects the political value of listening to the public.'

If health care is increasingly something beyond personal responsibility, then it is also something which seems to be beyond the ordinary rules of life, something to which people think there should be no limit. As authorities throughout the country struggle to improve the service by streamlining and rationalizing, by closing down the old, out of date and dangerous, they are met with great hostility from the general public. As David Ennals said wistfully, 'it is impossible to close down any hospital, anywhere, for whatever reason'. Not all closures are rational and we are quite right to question them, but sometimes there are good reasons which we, in the heat of the moment, fail to consider or which we might not even like. We don't like the universal move to close down out-of-date or isolated maternity units and convert them for use by old people, despite the fact that they might actually be dangerous. We would like the old maternity units, however inconvenient, to remain open, and if we have to put old people somewhere, well, build them something new. A community physician faced with this problem in an industrial town noted ironically that those who became most heated about the proposed switch were acting against their own individual best interests.

'There's all these people on the streets collecting signatures to stop us closing the obstetric unit but the people who are signing will never need maternity care. They'll all need geriatric care before long. The local press are not sympathetic to us either. They highlight what the local community sees as important. Basically they want to preserve what they already have, and if there are deficiencies they think we should build afresh.'

This kind of informal, impromptu expression of public feeling about the health service is traditional becáuse, in the past, the public's opinion on matters of health and its organization has not been formally sought. Indeed, the impression has long been given that the public's opinion is not all that welcome. Many a patient in hospital has been made to feel that the place would run a great deal better without him. In many ways lay people are still not welcome in the health service, but lay opinion has now been built into the new order of things. Since reorganization the opportunity has been there for public participation in health to be active and forward-looking, rather than reactive. A large body of medical opinion lumps the new Community Health Councils together with the administration as part of the regrettably large body of ignorant lay opinion that now has a chance to meddle in concerns that should be the sole province of the expert. Considering what experts are capable of doing with our money when given their head, there is something to be said for public opinion, however ignorant, at least having the chance to question what goes on in its name and with its taxes. If the public is ignorant then it is up to the health service to be a great deal less secretive and protective about what goes on inside it, and to supply CHCs (Community Health Councils) with the information that will enable them to take a more comprehensive and educated view of any issue in question.

Community Health Councils exist in each Health District, 207 in all. They have a statutory right to be consulted on all plans for the health service in their district, and to keep an eye on the far-reaching decisions that may be made on health services within their particular region. They do this with varying degrees of success. They have the right – frequently exercised – to object and to hold up plans. In some places they confine themselves to daily trivia such as what patients eat for breakfast, and they don't meddle with what they don't understand. In others they object to everything on principle without applying the reasonable use of information. However this system works in its infancy, it is healthy for people within the health service to be forced to explain and justify the decisions they take which affect us all. And likewise, it is good for at least one section of the public to be forced to look at all the complex issues involved in providing a health service rather than simply acting on emotion.

The last point would carry more weight if Community Health Councils didn't tend to be made up of exactly those people who always were on committees and always will be. The basic failure of Community Health Councils is in representing the public point of view, simply because the public as a whole is not interested enough to go to its meetings or to lobby it with its ideas. 'On average,' said the secretary of a comparatively lively CHC, 'we'll get half a dozen people at a meeting, unless it's a crisis issue. We had a meeting on the closing of a local convalescent home and sixty people turned up to that – an emotive issue will really pull them in. We had a meeting on abortion in the Town Hall and we had to call the police to control the crowds.'

Crowds do not usually gather when the public are asked to

participate in any form of long-term government planning. At
ten public meetings about future hospital planning in Clwyd the
total public attendance came to 330 people, 200 of whom came
to only two meetings which happened to have been about a
proposed hospital closure. The normal attendance was less than
20 people.[4] In consequence, Community Health Councils have
tended to be monopolized by the same people who have been
riding a particular hobby-horse for years and have become experts at it. Officially the breakdown of membership of a Community Health Council is 50% local authority appointments,
33% from voluntary organizations with a special interest in
health and social services, and the rest appointed by the region.
In practice, as one member darkly said, 'CHCs were set up to
be wide open for takeover by anyone who wants to.' From the
administrators' point of view, CHCs can be a positive help, or
they can be a pestilential nuisance. They have power without responsibility,' said one, 'and they are jumping on the backs of
people who have more and more responsibility and less and less
power. CHCs are bound to be fairly parochial. There's lots of
pressure groups who go to them with an interest in grabbing
headlines.'

'The spectrum of attention and activity from CHCs is
tremendous,' said another. 'Some are so quiescent you never
hear from them. Others see themselves as creators of policy, as
moulders of public opinion but they don't consult the public.
We have one CHC in the region which is fighting us over plans
to reshape the service. They're very much opposed to health
cuts in any form and they've got the whole region tied up with
different branches of the health service fighting each other instead of getting anything done. In other areas they supply extra
power to the service and they can be very useful.'

Not many people are prepared to help the CHCs find a role.
The public remains indifferent except when highly emotive
issues are involved. The full-time professionals resent having to
take them into account except when they think that the CHC
might help them in lobbying for some pet project. Council
members themselves lack the confidence needed to commit

themselves on priorities because they often feel they lack the necessary information and they don't get the right help from the doctors and administrators involved. They also tend to react instantly on individual issues rather than take the problems of the health service as a whole into account. Members of CHCs are more aware of the problems of giving reliable advice and taking considered decisions than many of the professionals like to think.

'It's a very difficult tightrope we walk,' said a CHC secretary. 'The worst frustration is seeing something very clearly from two different angles. We see it from the regional angle when it is thought that something is impossible, and we see from the patient angle how stupid this official view is. We're just piggies in the middle. We have got to accept the reasoned arguments from the authorities – and I mean reasoned, not just financial. But we've also got to look at the general public's point of view. The authorities here accept what we're trying to do on behalf of the general public even if they think it's misguided. How an individual Council works depends very much on the secretary and the individual members. One of our problems is that some of our members are very strong on one particular issue. We can be manipulated by anybody. Then more and more people come to complain to us. Five people will come to me with complaints and I will advise them to write to the Family Practitioner Committee and they say they will. I then get in touch with the FPC to see what's happened and I find nobody has complained. I have acted as a safety valve which is fine, but those complaints were genuine. By acting as a safety valve, have we allowed a situation to continue?'

And by acting as a channel for public reaction and opinion, is the CHC being used to direct it safely to boggy and infertile ground? Is the CHC a sop towards public participation but nothing more? The idea is that CHCs should act as a powerful public forum, but if the power comes from the people, the current is low. A recent national survey of CHCs showed that membership is predominantly middle class, middle-aged, professional and male, with consequent reflection of middle class, middle-aged interests. The capacity of CHCs to be dynamic is certainly limited. In a study on *CHCs in Action* published by the Nuffield Provincial Hospitals Trust, J. Hallas wrote:

Change is not brought about by planning. In the whole history of ideas, any group which is criticized by another group has sought to dull the critical edge by taking the critics into membership. It would be a mistake for us to give up the power we have got by allowing this to happen. We must find collective strength and find structured ways of using it.[5]

In order for CHCs to be more effective as the voice of the public in the health service it seems that information is the key. Given more resources, CHCs could be extremely useful collators of evidence and information on local health services, information which could be useful both as ammunition for the public and for health service planners. If there is a lesson for the members of CHCs and for individual members of the public it is to ask, ask and ask again. Where individual specialized voluntary groups are successful it is in the pooling of knowledge and the development of specialized information. Where users get the most out of the health service is where they are the best informed, and thus the best equipped, to get what they want out of an amorphous service. Where Community Health Councils are best equipped to argue their case is where they know what they are talking about. An inquiring and argumentative public is still the best protection against an apathetic and introspective service.

9 Changing the Face of Medicine

The shape of every health service is dominated by the demands of acute, technological medicine. It seems to be what we, the public, want most and it is certainly what the people who provide it have learned to give, but there is a very vocal body of opinion who say that this bias is all wrong, that the way to get value for money in the health service is to stand this pyramid on its head and spend far more time, energy and money on preventing illness than on curing it. The people who work in preventive health like to illustrate their value with little images and fables. They are the fence at the edge of the cliff which stops people falling over and thus prevents the need for an expensive rescue and ambulance service. One specialist in the diseases of civilization likes to make his point with a specially drawn slide showing two men diligently mopping up a floor which is being constantly flooded by a fully running tap. Although their lives are being taken up by the demands of the overflow, neither of them ever thinks of turning off the tap.

'These men are experts in floor-mopping-up,' says the lecturer. 'They have spent ten years of their life earning degrees in floor-mopping-up. They know everything there is to know about floor-mopping-up. Except how to turn off the tap.'

In most societies it is the floor-moppers-up who win the titles, the letters after their name, the plaudits, the prestige and the money. Tap-turners-off get few thanks. They receive very little public recognition, little professional kudos, few merit awards and large fees, and very little in the way of financial support for their work. Floor-moppers-up – to mix a metaphor – make a career out of first aid. It is they who put Humpty Dumpty together again. Tap-turners-off try to hold him on the wall or stop him getting up there in the first place. It is dull work. It makes their arms ache. No one can see them do it and if they fail and he falls, then all the king's horses and all the king's men come galloping gloriously in and get all the credit for the last-minute rescue. And yet if any society could work out a way to switch valuable resources into preventing diseases, stopping accidents, motivating the general public to care more about maintaining good health, a great many king's men and horses could be pensioned off.

The responsibility for balancing the needs of the individual whose life might be saved by acute medicine with the needs of the community whose collective lives may not be improved by it by one jot, rests with the comparatively young speciality of community medicine. Community medicine is concerned with the pattern of ill health in the community as a whole, not with the individual patient, and from the community physician's epidemiological viewpoint the problems of the health service look very different from those seen by a specialist in surgery or cardiology. The dominance of curative medicine has warped our whole concept of what health care can do and it tends to obscure the fact that the best way to good health is, regardless of the power of modern medicine, simply not to get ill in the first place. Nothing has a smaller statistical effect on a country's health indices than the quantity and quality of its health services. The community physician is very well aware of this, a fact which makes him a rather rare creature; a doctor with a built-in sense of his own superfluity. And yet the record of community medicine or, as it used to be known, public health, is an impressive one.

Most of the great improvements in health over the last hundred years have been due almost entirely to measures not associated with acute medicine. Infectious diseases have lost most of their terrors because of improvements in sanitation and clean water supplies and vaccination programmes. Improvements in nutrition, in industrial cleanliness and safety, in traffic speed limits and quality and quantity of housing, have lifted the whole quality of life for the community and transformed expectancy of life as well. In Britain in 1838 infant mortality was 150 per 1,000 births. Now it is 15·9. And life expectancy, which a hundred years ago was 41 for a man and 45 for a woman, is now 69·2 for men and 75·6 for women. The enormous difference made by social class and background proves that economic and social factors have more effect on health and life expectancy than medical care. A gentleman in London in 1844 had exactly twice the life expectancy of a common labourer. A gentleman in Leeds could expect to reach 44 while the labourer might reach 19, and in Liverpool the figures were 35 and 15.[1] These kind of discrepancies still exist and they are still related to life-style. One of the most vivid illustrations of this is the comparison carried out in the United States between the neighbouring states of Utah and Nevada.[2] The citizens of the two states have the same income levels, the same level of available medical care but very different levels of health and mortality. In Nevada, the state which is famous for Las Vegas and very little else, infant mortality is 40% higher than in Utah, the state which is the home of the religious and plain-living Mormons. The difference in life expectancy for adults is also between 40 and 50%. The main differences between the inhabitants of the two states lie in their stability and life-style. Mormons do not smoke or drink and they lead stable home lives. Only 10% of Utah's citizens are single, widowed, divorced or separated, compared with over 20% in Nevada. In 1970, 63% of Utah's adult residents had been born in their home state. In Nevada the figure was only 10% – Nevadans are most recent immigrants and their way of life is correspondingly more rootless and less healthy.

Once upon a time the young were carried away by diphtheria and measles and scarlet fever. Nowadays we suffer from an epidemic of violent accidents. In the United States three out of every four deaths in men between the ages of 15 and 25 are due to violence of some kind, to car accidents, suicide, murder. The rate of deaths due to accidents, half of which are traffic accidents, is twenty times higher than the death rate of a polio epidemic. In Britain we spend £500 million a year on patching ourselves up after road accidents, and over £100 million to treat smoking-related complaints. Even if we escape a road accident or cancer we are still prey to another modern epidemic, worry. In 1973 alone there were 46 million prescriptions issued for tranquillizers, enough to pacify the entire British Isles for a day or two. When the Health Education Council carried out research to discover what health issues concerned people most, they found that apart from the problems special to age and sex, everybody but everybody was worried about worry. Stress was the predominant problem in everyone's lives whether it took the form of worry about school, friction with parents, despair at the political situation, depression over unemployment and redundancy or money. In order to help combat this national gloom the Health Education Council launched a big campaign aimed at getting people to take more exercise, reasoning that if they promoted physical exercise at least people might sleep better and worry less.

This kind of lateral thinking may be what is needed from us all as conventional medical care reaches a point of no return. In order to have any great effect on the current mortality and morbidity rates our attitudes as to what health and ill health are would have to be radically changed. We may have to give up the passive model of health care, the one where we get wheeled through on a trolley and exciting, if alarming, things are done to us by men in white coats. We either have to allow the government to tell us how to behave, which is something nearly all of us find objectionable, or we have to take the initiative and do something for ourselves by looking critically at the way we live. On the largest scale this means taking social and political measures to reduce the incidence of ill health by improving the quality of life in other ways than by providing a large quantity of curative medicine. One inexplicable fact that bears closer inspection, for example, is that few factors have more bearing on the level of health in a community than the level of general education. An American study showed that if you tried to predict which men in their thirties would die within ten years, their educational level had more predictive power than their social class, job, family status or income.[3] In the United States children born to white mothers with eight years of schooling or less have twice the mortality rate of those born to mothers with twelve years of school or more.[4] Nobody knows why this is so, but a government that wished to improve the health of its people might be able to make a good case for injecting extra money into the educational system rather than into the health service.

Emotional stability is another factor which has a great effect on our physical health. Married people have better health and live longer than the divorced, widowed or single. The death rate of widowed and divorced men from suicide, motor accidents, cirrhosis of the liver and lung cancer – all behaviourally related conditions – is much higher than from conditions which are not so closely related to behaviour. Boredom is a threat to health as well as loneliness. Absence from work through sickness is much higher in those areas with a tradition of monotonous manual labour than among professional people, who not only have a higher degree of job satisfaction, but work in more pleasant surroundings with much greater freedom of movement. If a management team could come up with a scheme that not only made work more cost-effective, but also much more interesting for the worker, it is quite likely that absenteeism would drop. In fact, when the Swedish car company Volvo revolutionized its assembly line by putting workers in small groups to manufacture an entire car from start to finish rather than watch the same process endlessly repeated, this was one of the happy results.

What we tend to forget, and what the dramatic power of modern medicine helps us forget, is that health isn't a constant positive factor that is somehow destroyed by demons in the air, or by purple clouds of germs. It is a perpetual balance of the individual with the environment that can be affected violently by a tip in either scale. For most of us the dangers of the environment have been reduced by the general rise in the standard of living, by the innumerable measures and inventions that protect us from cold, hunger and disease. These have been replaced to some extent by different environmental threats like pollution and noise, but none the less the scale of health is dipping down more on the side of the individual these days. It is what we do and the way in which we behave that is emerging as the biggest threat to health. Modern epidemics have their roots in behaviour, in diet, in life-style, in mental attitudes, and few things could have more effect on health now than a conscious change in the way we live. Health is threatened by behaviour which weakens our resistance to external attack, by eating too much, by exercising too little, by dieting too much or too little, by drinking too much, by smoking, by losing control over our body weight, by not having enough sleep to restore ourselves, by driving too fast, or too carelessly or under the influence of alcohol. Health is threatened by stress and boredom, by social isolation and loneliness. If anyone were to sit down and ask how society, through a national health service, could best minimize the cause and effect of ill health in the community all these factors would have to be taken into account before anyone laid the foundation stone of a single hospital. These are the kind of considerations that must be taken into account in countries with negligible health services and very low budgets to spend on health. They must consider whether it is wise to spend thousands of pounds on treating children for gastro-enteritis if they return to villages which have no sanitation and to families who have no basic knowledge of hygiene, and succumb once more.

The biggest killer in the West today is ischaemic heart disease, or 'the coronary', which accounts for 43% of all male deaths between the ages of 45 and 64 in Britain. At the moment ischaemic heart disease occupies 3,500 hospital beds a day in Great Britain but despite the complexity of its causes there is a general agreement that it is a condition which is closely related to personal behaviour. A cardiac specialist writing in *World Medicine* complained about the illogical way in which we approached this disease. He pointed out that the mortality from ischaemic heart disease had fallen by 20% in the United States in the last eight years, partly due to a deliberate and conscious change in the eating and smoking habits of the average American. Its treatment, once it reaches the acute stage, involves either heavy drug therapy with beta blockers or extremely expensive surgery but, as this particular specialist pointed out, the evidence in favour of either of these courses of treatment improving survival in ischaemic heart disease is inconsistent and inconclusive. One of the factors which works against greater concentration on prevention of the disease is that doctors, as this surgeon points out, 'are trained to deal with sick people and our neglect of preventive medicine can therefore be understood if not entirely condoned'. But the bill for this bias to medicine may be too high. Why should we pay for expensive by-pass surgery while patients continue to be reckless in their diet and unhealthy in their habits? It is known that people who smoke and manage to give it up actually reduce their risk of having a coronary attack. It is also known that the other main risks associated with ischaemic heart disease are obesity, lack of exercise, high blood pressure and high blood fat levels – all of which could be inter-related and all of which could be under the control of the individual himself. The government consultative document[5] *Prevention and Health: Everybody's Business* states:

To the extent therefore that coronary heart disease is determined by a man's life-style, the prime responsibility for his own health falls on the individual. The role of the health professions and of government is limited to ensuring that the public have access to such knowledge as is available about the importance of personal habit on health and that at the very least no obstacles are placed in the way of those who decide to act on that knowledge.

This last sentence brings up perhaps the most vexed question concerned with preventive health – how do you provide it effectively? Since the crux of the problem is getting the individual to control his own health, how does a health service reach that individual and obtain his cooperation? There is a very fine line to be walked between what most people would consider sensible public health measures, and what they consider gross interference. Fluoridation of the water supply is a case in point. At a cost of no more than a few pence per head per year, dental decay could be reduced by 50% or more, and yet public resistance to fluoridation is high. It seems to constitute an interference with personal liberty and conjure up visions of all kinds of other nasty things being added to the water. The compulsory wearing of seat belts is another illustration of strong resistance to government interference in personal behaviour although it has been calculated that 14,000 fatal and serious injuries, and their consequent charge on the NHS would be avoided if everyone wore them.

Prevention works best where the desire of the government and the health service to act in a situation coincides with desire from the public to be controlled. Family planning is one area where the government and the people are in agreement, although it is easy to find countries where they are not. However, in Britain, the desire of the government to control population growth and thereby alleviate the social problems arising from large families and unwanted children, coincides happily with the desire of single girls to avoid pregnancy and of families to limit their size. The social cost of too many children is impossible to estimate, although a look at the strain on social services, on housing, on the job market, on mental health and family breakdown indicates its size. In financial terms the health service can quite easily balance the actual cost of having a baby against the cost of providing family planning services. In July 1976 over 90% of GPs were providing family planning services to two and three-quarter million women, with a further million being seen in special family planning clinics and hospitals. The cost of this service is £40 million, but the estimated burden on the health service arising from a hospital birth is £3,600. The Department of Health estimates that the service has already paid for itself.

Related services in antenatal care form one of the most important and effective areas of preventive medicine. As more and more antenatal classes and facilities are available to pregnant women the government's main concern is to see that they are used. The perinatal death rate is nearly five times higher in children of mothers who are late in seeing their doctors, than it is in those women who begin their antenatal care at the onset of pregnancy. Despite this, one large Welsh hospital reported that only 50% of its expectant mothers attended its course of antenatal classes. And yet the conscious effort to make childbirth safer for mother and child has resulted in a maternal death rate of one in 10,000 births compared with between 40 and 45 deaths per 10,000 in the early 1930s. It is noticeable, and it is not unique to antenatal care, that the women who take advantage of the care and information given to them and who present themselves for regular checks are the middle class, competent, self-aware women who might be thought to be in least need of the services offered. Not only can antenatal care keep a close surveillance on the mother's general health, and keep her informed on the best ways to ensure a safe pregnancy and birth, but the use of sophisticated screening techniques in pregnancy play a large part in detecting handicap in the unborn child, and in alerting obstetricians to risks while there is time to avert them.

The maternity services offer an excellent example of the two main directions in which preventive medicine can now go. On the one hand there is what might be called preventive medicine as an extension of technological medicine, or screening. Screening is the process by which otherwise healthy sectors of the population are tested for the presence of a condition which might otherwise go undetected until it was too late to do anything about it. Screening usually involves the paraphernalia of sophisticated equipment, laboratory tests and highly skilled technicians to use them, and although the aim of screening is to use the health services more effectively by catching treatable conditions in the early stages, screening misapplied can be extremely expensive. On the other hand there is the effective use of health education with a receptive and motivated audience. Few groups of prospective patients are more receptive than pregnant women to the need to be in good health, and to protect the health of the unborn child. Consequently most pregnant women soak in information about their condition like a sponge, whether it is true and helpful, or simply a lot of old wives' tales. The effective use of screening and the effective use of health education together are what have helped to make childbirth safer.

A good example of the selective use of screening to detect a condition is the use of amniocentesis to detect unborn children with Down's syndrome, or mongolism. A needle is inserted through the wall of the uterus and some of the amniotic fluid is withdrawn for testing. The presence of an odd chromosome in cells cultured from the fluid indicates that the foetus is affected. Because the procedure involves sophisticated laboratory testing and highly trained staff it is a very expensive one. The actual test costs only £80 to perform, but if it were to be performed on every single pregnant woman, that one test alone would account for about £64,000,000 a year. The risks of Down's syndrome increase with the age of the mother and are at their highest in mothers over the age of 40. It still costs £8,000 per case detected in mothers over 40 but if it were extended to mothers under 30, the cost could be £80,000 per case detected. Into the complicated sums that lie behind health service decisions go the costs that would be incurred if the handicapped child survived: £2,000 a year to stay in a mental-handicap institution, £1,000 a year for special education. For mothers of 40 and over, the costs of keeping the likely number of mongol children to survive outweigh the costs of detection and subsequent abortion decided on by the mother. For younger mothers the sums do not balance so favourably.

Unfortunately screening has become fashionable and demand has increased without this kind of reflection and cost-benefit being done. The demand for the screening of healthy people in the private sector has produced a profitable business. The NHS, with cost and benefit to weigh up, cannot afford to be seduced by public demand into carrying out a vast number of useless screening tests. As people have more and more experience of screening, a set of criteria have been developed for its use. The World Health Organization publication *Principles and Practice of Screening for Disease* suggests that:

1. The condition sought should be an important health problem.
2. There should be an accepted treatment for patients with the recognized disease.

3. Facilities for diagnosis and treatment should be available.
4. There should be a recognizable latent or early symptomatic stage.
5. There should be a suitable test or examination.
6. The test should be acceptable to the population.
7. The natural history of the condition including development from latent to declared disease should be adequately understood.
8. There should be an agreed policy on whom to treat as patients.
9. The cost of case-finding, including diagnosis and treatment of patients diagnosed, should be economically balanced in relation to possible expenditure on medical care as a whole.
10. Case-finding should be a continuous process and not a once for all project.

It will be seen that this highly specific definition of effective screening is very different from the popular idea of screening as a kind of universal sieve which lets through the healthy and catches up the incipiently ill. It is also very different from the application of screening in the private sector as a 10,000 mile service to be carried out on anyone who wants it. While it is undeniable that a person who has been screened in this way and comes out clear feels a lot better for it, a health service has to ask if this is enough. There is a reverse side to screening which means that as well as detecting early signs of a curable condition, it may also indicate unnecessary treatment. Innumerable studies have shown that if you go out and look for symptoms of illness in an apparently healthy population you will find them. A screening programme is an automatic promise from its organizers that if it finds anything then treatment will follow. At any given time, as we have seen, a section of population screened will come up with the symptoms of something or other. Since this 'Clinical Iceberg', as it is known, is normally content to rest oblivious beneath the surface, one can only assume that many of these symptoms either cause no trouble, or depart as inconspicuously as they arrived; that a vast proportion of abnormality simply cures itself.[6] One of the problemes thrown up by mass screening for various conditions from TB to cervical cancer, is that early detection picks up symptoms which might fade in time, and encourages expensive treatment in cases which might cure themselves or which, in any case, obviously fail to disturb the people who have them. The danger here is of unnecessary and often drastic treatment such as hysterectomy, for example. Going out into the community to seek out ill health among a generally healthy population not only creates invalids out of large numbers of people who thought of themselves as passably fit, but it puts a direct, immediate and very expensive onus on to an overworked health service to do something about the problems they uncover.

Nevertheless public demand for screening services is high. The popular belief is that screening is a public benefit which would help to keep us all healthier at a lower cost. Very few studies into the advantages of screening have been carried out, and those that have fail to prove its value. One in particular, which was carried out in south-east London, seems to come down strongly against it as a cost-effective way of providing preventive care.[7] The South-East London Screening Study, set up by St Thomas's Hospital and the General Practice, St Paul's Cray, took 7,229 people aged between 40 and 64 and allocated them randomly into two groups. The first group were given two general health screenings within two years, and conditions discovered were followed up. The other group received no screening. The idea behind the trial was to see if a GP based screening service would be a valuable extension of the NHS, both in producing a healthier population and in saving money. Five years later the groups underwent a survey which showed no difference between them. Nine years later they were surveyed again, and again there was found to be no significant difference. And yet it was estimated that if a similar service were to be set up universally throughout the NHS the cost would be £142 million. The only other long-term study into the results of across-the-board health screening was carried out by the Kaiser Permanente Group in California and it too failed to find any significant difference between groups of patients who were screened and groups who weren't.[8] After seven years only three of sixty statistical tests carried out on their patients came up with any significant results – two in favour of the screened group and one against – but this result is the same as one would expect to find purely by chance.

And yet there is no doubt that a generalized screening service like this would be extremely popular, not so much from the advantages that might come from having a condition discovered and treated, as from the relief at finding oneself to be perfectly healthy – officially. A GP who disapproves of general check-ups on perfectly healthy, symptomless patients was badgered by one of his patients into giving him one. The doctor charged the patient a deterrent £10, explaining that he didn't see why the patient should have a useless procedure carried out on the NHS. The patient proved to be as healthy as the doctor thought and he said, smiling as he counted out his money, that it was the best £10 worth he had ever had in his life. But can the health service afford to hand out screening tests as placebos – or can it afford to treat all the abnormalities uncovered? Screening can dig up its own brand of trouble in the form of false positives – those cases which look as though they present symptoms and require further investigation but turn out to be negative – and false negatives – those cases which appear to be negative but later prove to have been undetected positive cases.

It seems that generalized screening is, as far as the health service goes, a very dubious proposition. Screening, then, must be of value in more specific cases, in the detection of certain pinpointed conditions among certain pinpointed sections of the public. But even here there are very real snags which have not yet been solved. One such case is the detection of cervical cancer by a smear test. Professor Cochrane's voice is not the only one which asks if the value of screening for cervical cancer has really been proved. Even more problematic is the use of screening in the detection of breast cancer, a condition which accounted for 11,775 deaths in 1970 and keeps 1,525 hospital beds occupied. About one in thirty women die from breast cancer. Such studies as have been done indicate that screening would be most effective applied to women in their fifties. If all women over 50 were eligible for a nationwide screening test there would be a possible response of 5·4 million women requiring tests at a cost of between £20 and £30 million a year. And yet 19 out of 20 women will never develop breast cancer. There is clearly more work to be done in narrowing down the group to be screened even further and such work is being done. If this group were successfully identified the cost per case detected could drop from £8,000 to around £2–3,000. In the meantime women who follow the advice beamed at them from women's magazines and newspapers can carry out a rudimentary screening test of their own by regularly examining their own breasts for unexpected lumps which might indicate malignant tissue.

Which brings us to the other aspect of preventive health care – personal responsibility encouraged by health education. Health education and awareness comes at us from various sources, from newspapers, television, magazines, books, friends and neighbours and last – and almost least – from the Health Education Council. This is somewhat unfair on the Health Education Council since its job is supplying information to schools and the media as well as directly to us through campaigns, but the meagre resources with which it is supplied are some indication of the importance it is given in competition with other branches of the health service. The competition facing it is very fierce indeed. In 1977 the Health Education Council spent £300,000 on anti-smoking propaganda while the tobacco manufacturers spent £40 million on advertising, especially on glamorous advertisements which subtly suggest that smoking is an intrinsic part of a healthy, sexy, wind-blown outdoor life. But the chief medical officer, Dr George Cust, nevertheless feels that the smoking battle is being won.

1957 was the first paper by Doll and Bradford Hill. The Medical Research Council said smoking was dangerous to health and nobody really believed it was true at the time. Now even smokers believe that smoking is dangerous. You've got to see things in longer periods of time. The anti-smoking campaign started in the late 1950s and smoking reached its highest point in 1960. If it had carried on at that rate we would have spent £327 million on smoking in 1976. Instead we spent £213 million. Social class one has dropped smoking more than social class five. 75% of doctors don't smoke. Lung cancer deaths are coming down in younger men – we're not going to affect older people. It takes time to change, it takes time for the results to come through and there's a long incubation period for the disease. Giving up smoking itself is very difficult. There is nicotine addiction and these people, when they give up, get withdrawal symptoms. Non-inhalers, oral gratifiers can give up fairly easily so perhaps the ones who've been giving up are the easy ones.

This is the problem facing any attempt at changing behaviour – people know what is bad for them but they still do it because they want to. There can hardly be anyone left who doesn't know that smoking harms your health, but smokers keep on smoking. We also know that it is bad for us to eat too much, to take too little exercise, to do without sleep, to drive too fast, yet we persist in doing all these things almost as a gesture of defiance against fate. We resent deeply any attempts by the government to interfere with what we regard as our personal concern but our habitual cry that it is our own business how we conduct our life has a logical flaw in it. We may resent attempts to make us wear seat belts but we would be appalled if the same government refused to treat our injuries if we were hurt as a result of breaking a seat belt law. We want the safety net. We regard it as an inalienable right for which we pay taxes, but we don't see why this should carry with it any obligation to go carefully on the high-wire. Figures show that 70% of the French eat too much, and that 50% of their hospital cases have some connection with the over-use of alcohol, but to a Frenchman his high food bills and his high consumption of wine are sacred.[9] Would he accept the risks of obesity and cardiac failure and alcoholism so cheerfully if his health service refused to treat diseases which were so clearly the result of his failure of personal responsibility?

Prevention is dull, but worse than dull – it interferes with our pleasures and freedoms. A deeply pessimistic view of the possibility of getting people to take some responsibility for their own health is built into the health budget of almost every Western country. A survey conducted from the United States to Russia showed that countries spent no more than 10 cents per person per year at most on health education and the promotion of preventive health measures.[10] Preventive health doesn't catch votes and it is even politically unpopular. The basic dilemma in the promotion of personal responsibility for health is how far the state should intervene. In general people take a perverse and determined pride in their individual freedom to die in their own way. Loud cheers are raised when public figures attack the 'nanny state' and proclaim their intention of smoking or driving themselves to death as they choose. And yet people can be motivated to change if the message is hammered into them long and loud enough. Social classes one and two make much better use of the health services and practise more preventive health and dental care than social classes three, four and five. Doctors, as we all know, have largely given up smoking because they know in a more vivid way than the rest of us that it can kill. The problem of the Health Education Council is partly that it lacks the funds to hammer the message home as heavily as it needs to be hammered. The message is there but the medium is lacking.

A reverse problem facing preventive health services is that when they do succeed in getting a message across they then fail to cope with the response. Just as screening can crash the health service into the Clinical Iceberg, so too much and too effective health education can swamp the service in its own way. A campaign conducted in Tyne Tees on alcoholism which encouraged people with a drink problem to present themselves for counselling and help, encouraged over 1,000 people to come forward and the services were unable to cope with the consequent demand for their help. The next time a campaign against alcoholism was conducted it stuck to the area of primary prevention, of boosting moderation rather than abstinence. Health education is also beginning to concentrate on the positive aspects of good health care rather than on awful warnings and admonitions. At the time of writing the Health Education Council's latest campaign is aimed at the promotion of fitness, exercise and self-help.

We decided to do a 'Look After Yourself' campaign with the emphasis on more exercise, a more reasonable diet, cutting down on fats, eating more fibre. Health education has always been very much 'don't smoke, don't drink'. This campaign is a positive one. 'Give up smoking' is a negative thing, but this is to make you feel better. Our problem is how to combat increasing stress spirals. It is silly, with a health service so curatively oriented, to let people smoke and drink themselves to death. The Germans have a programme called 'Trim' and the Canadians have a national keep-fit programme. So do Holland, Scandinavia, the Americans – all with a reasonable take-up. We see the GPs wanting a partnership with people – it goes back to Beveridge. He saw a lot of self-help in the system.

There is evidence from many sources that when people take a hand in their own care, when self-help means self-maintenance rather than simply treating yourself from the local chemist, that the results are good. A study carried out on 7,000 residents of Alameda County, California, shows that men and women aged 45 who follow six or seven of the following health rules have a life expectancy of between eleven and seven years longer than those who only follow fewer than four.[11] The secret of longevity in Alameda County – and presumably elsewhere – is to eat regularly and not between meals, to eat breakfast, to get between seven and eight hours, sleep each night, to keep a normal weight, not to smoke, to drink moderately, to exercise regularly. Very simple measures and very effective ones, but measures that must be self-imposed, not enforced from outside. Well-to-do Americans, who are much more diet conscious than the British, have also succeeded in reducing the rate of coronary heart disease by halving their cholesterol intake and thus reducing the average cholesterol intake by between 5 and 10%, so that coronary heart disease is slowly becoming the disease of the poor rather than the affluent. The overall mortality rate from ischaemic heart disease in America dropped below 200 deaths per 100,000 in 1976, its lowest level in 35 years.

Changing diet is one simple personal measure we could all take to improve our health. The booming commercial success of the health food business is one indicator of the guilt that we already harbour on the subject. Deep in many of us is the suspicion that we should be eating better, or more, or less or vegetarian. We spend an estimated £20 million on laxatives in Britain each year, and in America the figure is 250 million dollars on top of doctors' prescriptions. If we ate the right foods all this expenditure might be unnecessary. Over-refined foods have eliminated the necessary fibre from our diet and slowed down the process of digestion. America has acknowledged this trend in its people's diet by setting up dietary goals for them to follow, the first of which is to take more of the daily calorie requirement in the form of unrefined carbohydrates. They are following through these good intentions by actually voting money to enforce the goals. Studies throughout the world show that diet has a dramatic effect on health, and that many of the modern epidemics are closely related to it. A small island in the Pacific Ocean which discovered that it was made of phosphates switched, in its new-found affluence, to a refined Western diet and 30% of its inhabitants now have diabetes. The Pima Indians of America who abandoned their traditional diet for the universal American fare of refined carbohydrates, popcorn and Cokes now have the highest incidence of diabetes and gallstones in the world. Diet experts who have been looking into the problem of the fibre-free diet and its effects on Western man have estimated that a mere spoonful of bran a day would be enough to halt the damage. Failing that, the consumption of wholemeal instead of white bread could be encouraged by a government subsidy on wholemeal flour, something that would cost a great deal less than the current investment into the treatment of all the diseases that are supposedly related to the absence of fibre – of coronary heart disease, varicose veins, haemorrhoids, appendicitis, diverticular disease of the colon, obesity and cancer of the large bowel.

The importance of preventive care, both in making the best use of the health service and in preserving the good health of the individual, is universally accepted. But it is the job of health education. Without motivation and cooperation from the general public, preventive measures run into the sand. The financial, medical and social benefits of a polio vaccination campaign have been estimated as being worth twelve times the cost of the actual immunization over twenty years. And yet one child in three is not taken for vaccination. Antenatal clinics and screening tests have had a profound effect on the well-being of the individual mother and child, and on mortality rates, but mothers continue to stay away from maternity services until it is too late. In the end, people cannot be forced into taking care of their own health – it must come from them – but they can be told and told and told, until the facts sink below the level that means action. It is no accident that general education is the factor most closely related to good health, that doctors give the least information to their worst informed patients, that the best educated sectors of the population make the best use of the service and take the most preventive health and dental care. Ultimately, a better use of the health service and better health for individuals rests on our own awareness and the responsibility of each one of us for our own and our family's health.

10 Paying the Piper

The preceding chapters have shown and illustrated some of the problems currently facing the health services, those who organize and work in them and those who use them. The worst of these problems spring from the insoluble conflict between a limitless demand and a limited supply, and they are not helped by the fact that the interests of medicine are different from the interests of a health service, or that the demand on acute services are so continued and so heavy that there simply isn't the breathing space to stop and re-examine the directions in which health services are going. This book has also looked at some of the ways in which these problems are being confronted, whether successfully or not, and at ways in which they might be tackled in the future. It has shown that the British National Health Service, despite the masochistic affection with which we regard its undoubted failings, is far from being alone in its troubles and crisis. What this chapter aims to show is that the NHS, battered, bedraggled and worn at the edges as it is, may even be uniquely well equipped to deal with these problems. Although it has been seen that massive injections of money are far from being the immediate and magic cure-all for the health service disease, payment for health – who pays, to whom, for what, who spends and who manages – is crucial to the successful reorganization of an inefficient health service.

One point should be made absolutely clear at the outset – no matter who receives the money, whether it is the individual physician, the insurance company, the hospital or the state, it is always the public who pays. There is no such thing as a free health service, there are simply different ways of charging the public for health care, and it has been estimated that the average family ends up paying the same share under any system. Most health services in the world are in a constant state of argument over which payment system to adopt in order to ensure the steadiest flow of funds into the service, the most equitable distribution of services throughout the country, the easiest way of lifting the burden on the sick individual, whether it is the debate in the United States over the introduction of national health insurance or the debate in Britain over the introduction of hospital charges and private insurance. No system is entirely satisfied with the efficiency of the method it has, and health service managers feel fondly that somewhere, over some distant hill, the pastures must be greener. The NHS itself is currently funded almost entirely from central taxation although a myth exists in people's minds that it comes from the National Insurance – or as it is often mistakenly called – the National Health Stamp. In fact National Insurance contributions account for only 8% of the NHS revenue. A further 2·5% comes from direct charges to patients and the rest comes from central government funds where it has to compete with equal demands from education, transport, roads, defence and so on. When it comes to getting money out of public funds the NHS learns to take its place with other national priorities.

At the end of the system the NHS still provides nearly all its services free of charge at point of contact to anybody who needs them. As we have seen this leads to various overt and covert ways of rationing health care in the face of a demand which the system cannot meet. One argument against this generosity which is often heard is that the provision of a free service leads to profligate use of it by the general public. There is no evidence of this and there is also no evidence that charging acts as a deterrent. Because the public is unaware of the real cost of the treatment and attention they receive, then the theory is that they practise no care in the demanding of it. Theoretically, if they knew that a course of treatment cost £1,000, then they might be more sparing in the use of it, but it is more likely, as one cynical health worker muttered, that if they knew there were two treatments, one costing £50 and the other costing £100, then they'd be encouraged to ask for the £100 treatment because they would assume it was better. In fact it is the doctor, not the patient, who is in control of costs. All the individual patient can do is to make an appointment with a doctor. After that point the course of events and train of expense is in medical hands. However, the idea persists that we would have a more economically used health service if charges were made directly on the public and that, if such charges were made, then there would be a limitless source of much needed income.

Despite all the other ways of improving the efficiency of a health service there is no doubt that more money would be a very welcome thing. The NHS is sitting on a backlog of old buildings and equipment that badly need replacing. Half of its patients are housed in hospitals built in the nineteenth century and under a fifth of its patients are in hospitals built in the last thirty years, since the beginnings of the service, despite hopes of a massive hospital building programme. A report by the Royal Institute of British Architects, quoted in the *British Medical Association's Evidence to the Royal Commission*, recommended that £100 million should be spent simply on maintenance. No wonder that everyone concerned with the provision of the health service wonders if there isn't some more profitable way of turning the public's money in its direction.

The way in which health services are paid for, and the way in which the public is charged, is a crucial problem which brings many other questions in its wake. What is involved is the delicate balancing of an equation with two equally important sides – what is the most equitable, efficient and socially just way of charging the consumer, and what is the most equitable, efficient and socially just way of providing the service? It is futile to look at one side of the payment problem without considering the other because much more is involved than the simple provision of a cornucopia of money to spend on medicine. The method of payment dictates the method of organization, and with a near unmanageable monster like the health business, it matters very much who is in control. The simplest and most direct way of paying for health care is by fee-for-service. The patient needs a doctor's attention. He goes to the doctor, gets the attention and pays a direct fee. There are slight variations on this system. In America some health maintenance organizations charge their consumers an annual premium but pay their physicians a fee for service. In the Mayo Clinic it works the other way. The physician gets an annual salary but the individual patient pays the organization a fee for service.

With fee-for-service the burden of payment falls directly and sometimes intolerably on the individual. The other ways of paying for health care represent different variations on spreading the load, either through private health insurance companies or through health maintenance organizations, or alternatively through national insurance schemes or general taxation. With private health insurance companies the individual, his family or his employer pays an annual premium which entitles the patient to certain benefits, the cost of which will be borne by the insurance company who usually pay the providers of the benefits by fee-for-service. Health maintenance organizations, which are increasingly popular in the United States, take a pool of patients who pay premiums and guarantee them health care provided by their own personnel so that people are paying as much for the guarantee of access to health care – a very important point where health care is unevenly distributed – as for financial cover in times of need. National insurance schemes for health guarantee the existence of a fund of money for that specific purpose but sometimes, when they continue to pay the providers of health care in the old ways, fail to operate any kind of control over the care provided and can, in their own way, contribute to medical inflation. Operating alongside insurance schemes which cover certain basic charges go extra charges – for prescriptions, dental care, hospital cars, hospital stay and so on. The administration costs of odd charges like these, and of the refundable fees payable in EEC countries, are very heavy, and although they may deter the patient from seeking care, they fail to deter the doctors from providing too much.

What is needed is a system which offers the maximum control over the quality and distribution of care at the same time as easing the burden of pay off the patient. Most of the current systems of payment fall short of this in some way or another, some dramatically so. Fee-for-service is something which doctors like because it means they are much better paid, but apart from acting as a deterrent to the individual patient who can't afford the fee, it also aids inflation by providing the incentive for unnecessary services. This is so whether the payment is made directly, or via private insurance or via some government scheme such as Medicare or Medicaid. One problem is that the direct purchaser of private health care, unlike any other class of consumer, has no way of knowing whether or not he is buying a pig in a poke. In no other area where money changes hands does the person buying the service have so little means of knowing whether he is getting value for money, whether the service is really necessary in the first place or whether it might be performed better elsewhere. The patient going for treatment under the NHS does at least know that the doctor will treat according to his medical, and not his financial need. The patient buying health in a private sector has no means of knowing whether the operation advised is necessary or not. All the evidence shows that when doctors make their money by selling units of medical care, then they make their decisions not entirely on the basis of medical need, but also on the basis of how many of those units they can sell. This is why the rates for non-urgent operations are higher in countries which operate on a fee-for-service basis. The number of hysterectomies performed in Saskatchewan jumped by 72% after the introduction of national health insurance which reimbursed the doctor.[1] In 1966, when Medicare and Medicaid were introduced in the United States, the volume of services given leapt as doctors and patients took advantage of the injection of new money.[2] It wasn't that more people were cared for, but that those that were got more care – more equipment, more operations, more tests – 75% more, but there has been no proof that the health of the nation was markedly improved. In one case study of breast cancer treatment in six Boston hospitals it was found that there was a 100% increase in cases receiving both surgery and radiation after 1966, but the percentage of patients who died within three years of treatment remained exactly the same.[3] Likewise, there were twice as many operations performed on a group of Federal employees covered by Blue Shield, which pays for fee-for-service, than on a similar insurance scheme which simply pays its doctors a flat salary.[4]

The American service shows what happens when medical services are left to run themselves on a purely commercial basis. Firstly, a large proportion of the population will be unable to provide cover for themselves and their families as costs of treatment, and insurance, rise astronomically out of the reach of the individual. An estimated 10 million Americans have no health insurance. Many of those who are insured have inadequate cover. Over one-third of bankruptcies in 1970 – 50,000 personal bankruptcies in all – were caused by inability to pay medical bills.[5] Medicine in America is now the largest industry in the country next to automobiles, and by 1980 it will be the largest. With the outlook of a cut-throat commercial industry it is beginning to hawk its wares as if they were automobiles or hamburgers. Competing hospitals have marketing directors and their aim is not to provide good health care where it is needed, but to fill beds, to sell surgery as if it were a consumer good like any other. Hospitals run at nearly 100% occupancy in order to keep the cash-flow healthy, though in the NHS that would be considered as breaking point on services and staff. The marketing director of one hospital in Philadelphia predicted that the time would come when hospitals and doctors would be advertising their services openly.

'In ten years time maybe they will do TV commercials. The consumer movement wants it that way. They are pressing us to publicize our rates and services. On top of that, costs are rising at such an astronomical speed that only hospitals that are as well run as successful businesses will survive the onslaught.' Already a hospital in Las Vegas is offering an all-expenses paid round trip to Las Vegas provided the consumer comes in for a spot of elective surgery while he is in town.

A final and serious disadvantage of medical care provided on private enterprise lines is that it offers no incentive anywhere along the line for the people who provide it to provide it equi-

G

tably. Access is one of the gravest problems which affects privately operated medical care since, as the system depends on private payment for its funding, it can only operate where the money is likely to be forthcoming. The problems of gaps in the service, which exist even in government-operated services, are exaggerated by the need to serve a comparatively affluent population, and by the need of the doctor who depends directly on his patients for his living to guarantee himself a reasonable income. The tendency of professional workers to gravitate to the most congenial, stimulating and best-off areas is encouraged, and where the individual doctors go, the health services follow. The competition inherent in such a system also works against the efficient provision of health services since it encourages rather than limits the building of too many expensive hospitals, the provision of the very latest and most costly – though maybe not tried and tested – equipment, the carrying out of innumerable tests, the prescribing of unlimited drugs. The existence of a free health service is supposed to encourage profligacy, but when people are paying a great deal for something, they like to see they get a lot for their money. Although a higher proportion of a country's Gross National Product may consequently be spent on health care, it is meaningless when it comes to indicating the quality of that care and the effect of it on the country's health. Private payment and insurance schemes which exercise no control over the providers also lead to serious neglect of the 'care' areas of the health service. The chronic sick, the old, the mentally ill and handicapped are not in a position to pay for long-term care, nor will insurance companies take on such an open-ended commitment for them. Consequently they are left defenceless in the face of a financial burden which nobody will take up for them and, in free enterprise systems just as in others, slide forgotten to the bottom of the pile. If even the NHS neglects these people and its caring role for the insistent demands of curative medicine, the situation in a less controlled health service is infinitely worse. Fee-for-service offers only cure not care.

Halfway-houses exist. Many of the European countries

finance their health services through a mixture of private payment and insurance schemes and taxation, but it must be said strongly that if insurance schemes only pay the bill without querying its necessity, then health inflation will never be brought under control. This is where a monopoly buyer of health care – a government which cushions the cost for its citizens and exercises controls over the providers of health care – has the potential to balance both sides of the equation. It has the power to supervise, change and encourage it: the ability to plan on the long term, to eliminate waste and control quality and, more than any other method of funding, it has the power to control cost. For all the faults of the National Health Service, state-run health care will monopolize the health services of the future as more and more governments see the need to exercise some control. Britain spends less of its GNP (Gross National Product) on health care than many other countries, not because it provides less health care but because it is in a position to control costs, as, for example, drug costs, where it is the monopoly buyer. Also, although many people find this hard to believe, its administration is cheaper. In Britain, general administration costs (excluding hospitals) account for only 2·6% of the budget as compared to France's 10·8%, Sweden's 7·6% or the United States 5·3%. As Rudolf Klein wrote in the *British Medical Journal*:

While the National Health Service may have an expensively elaborate managerial structure, it is outstandingly efficient in terms of collecting and distributing funds ... because it collects its money very cheaply through the tax system instead of working through insurance companies or funds, and does not make a multiplicity of individual charges and reimbursements. So any move towards a system based on fees, charges, or insurance seems ... certain to increase the number of bureaucrats and the costs of administration.

The administration costs of the British United Provident Association, the largest of the private health insurance agencies in Britain, are 10%. This is because any system which involves reimbursement is very expensive in bureaucracy – hence the high cost of the French health service which refunds the cost of treatment to its patients. BUPA (British United Provident Association) is, as might be expected, in favour of a mixed health service, one which offers a private option alongside a state service. This idea of a two-tier system – a government service which provides for the indigent, the old, for children, for the chronic sick and handicapped – and a private system for those able to fund themselves, is a very popular one. Supporters of private care are in favour of it for obvious reasons, but so are supporters of the NHS because they mistakenly believe that it would relieve some of the burden which the service currently finds so hard to bear. If private care were to be increased in Britain it could only operate in a two-tier system because private health agencies are quite incapable of carrying the heavy cost of chronic illness and long-term dependency. In a very minor way the two-tier system already operates in Britain where private health care is available alongside the NHS but the two are so inextricable, the private sector being very heavily dependent on the public one, as to be almost inseparable. There are some advantages to a private sector. There are times when the most dedicated supporter of public transport – knowing it to be an excellent thing, even while he acknowledges its inefficiency in practice – will be tempted, while standing at a bus stop in the rain, to hail a taxi, so the private health sector in Britain acts as a kind of taxi service alongside the public network of the NHS, with all its excellence in principle and its failings in practice.

The advantages of private care in Britain are offered *because* we have a National Health Service on which it depends. Independent medicine in Britain is far from independent. The most fiercely fought battle within the health service has been over the retention of pay-beds within NHS hospitals. Absolute commitment to some form of private option on the one hand, supported by those doctors who gain a great deal of extra income from their private patients, struggles with absolute commitment to public medicine on the other, particularly from the health service unions who find the social divisions enforced by a two-tier system morally offensive. The battle to remove pay-beds from within NHS hospitals is an important one, partly as a matter of principle in separating the private sector from the NHS, and also because it would pose such practical difficulties to the private sector. Most of the beds used by private patients are actually inside the NHS even though they are being slowly cut back. Private health insurance schemes are busy building to rectify their loss, but how possible is it, in a system where 95% of medicine is practised within the public sector, to buy oneself out, and what advantage is there when the state has promised to provide health care at absolutely no charge to every citizen in need of it?

Over two million people subscribe to BUPA, and according to BUPA's own publicity, the advantages of private health care are speed and convenience. The private patient jumps over the heads of those on the lengthy NHS waiting lists, and gets the guaranteed attention of his own consultant and the privacy of his own room. BUPA's own provision of private nursing homes had a total of 740 beds at the last count and they relied on the use of some 4,000 NHS pay-beds (out of 400,000 beds in NHS hospitals). The people who subscribe to private health schemes in Britain tend increasingly to be company employees who get the cover as part of a block insurance taken out by their employers. The number of individuals insuring themselves is dropping all the time. Apart from the use of NHS beds, private medicine also relies on NHS doctors. An estimated £12 million in private medical fees is distributed among 6,000 NHS doctors in return for work on private patients. Of the total insurance payments, 48% goes on medical fees and 44% goes on hospital costs, 84% of which goes to the NHS. The amount of money that comes in to the NHS from private practice is less than 1% of its total budget – £58 million in 1976.

These figures are all very well, but when it comes to finding out exactly who goes in for private practice and who doesn't the information is much harder to come by. An administrator who tried to measure the extent of private practice within his area, a comparatively wealthy corner of the Home Counties with easy access to the best London hospitals, found it almost impossible. 'We have 56 private beds here,' he said, 'and we're closing 16.

They never have more than 50% occupancy, but then we know that the consultants here use the London hospitals. You can't study private medicine in this country. People get very cagey about it. I once tried to study private patients within this area and I met with a deathly silence. Consultants simply don't like to talk about it.'

Membership of the insurance schemes buys their subscribers a varying range of benefits according to contribution scale, region and so on. The cost of a room in a private wing can be nearly £300 a week in London, much less than that in a small country town. The private patient is buying the icing on the cake. If he really has something urgently the matter with him only the most fanatical supporter of private health care will deny that he will get very good treatment within the NHS. He may think that he is buying the best medical care, but the doctor treating him will almost certainly be a doctor he could see equally well on the NHS. What he is actually paying for is personal convenience and privacy. If he is cared for in a private NHS bed, he won't even get the glossy standard of luxury that the pictures in the insurance company brochures will have led him to expect.

'The private patients have got high expectations,' said one hospital. 'They may feel they're paying for colour telly, flowers, choice of menu and so on, but all they really get is the services of their consultant and time.'

'For what we charge,' said another, 'all you're really getting is a private bed. You get a napkin on your tray. You get green crockery instead of white, but it's the same NHS menu that all the other patients get.'

What the private patient in Britain is really buying is time. He can pay to jump the queue. He can fix the time to go in for a non-urgent operation, and it is this service that companies are really buying for their staff when they become members of group insurance schemes. Whether the private patient actually gets better medical care is a controversial issue. There is a large body of medical opinion that says he doesn't. Some doctors say that if there was anything really wrong with them they would rather be nursed in a busy public ward than tucked away in a private room with nobody to keep an eye on them, no twenty-four-hour medical coverage and none of the plethora of back-up services and emergency supplies that are available in a NHS hospital. A private patient may get the services of his chosen consultant at the actual time of operation but his nursing and after-care may be inadequate. A private room with a telephone is no substitute for the frequent check of a nurse or a pint of blood when you need it.

These practical objections to private medicine are quite apart from the moral objections, which are considerable. We have already seen that health care is a commodity in very short supply, and a commodity, moreover, that is not a luxury. At the moment we have a system where, by and large, the vast majority of the population receive health care according to medical need and not according to their bank balance. As long as private health care in Britain is so closely bound in with the state system each purchase of treatment directly deprives someone lower down the scale of treatment on the NHS. The inequalities of the NHS pose quite enough problems without intensifying them by the introduction of a free market. The seal of approval to the existence of private medicine within a state system was given, unwillingly, by Aneurin Bevan in 1948 when, in order to keep the best doctors within the health service he allowed them to keep private beds in NHS hospitals. Without the continued support of the NHS and the use of its staff, private medicine in Britain would be in a critical condition. It depends entirely on the state to train its doctors and, more important, to give them all the practice and experience they need on state patients before they acquire the necessary expertise and reputation to attract fee-paying patients. You don't see many junior doctors in private practice. They depend on the state to invest in the physical plant, the buildings and expensive equipment with which investigations and operations on fee-paying patients are carried out. If the private sector had to build up its own health service from scratch it would be quite unable to. By giving part of their time to private practice, part-time consultants are directly depriving NHS patients of their attention and helping to build up the very waiting lists that make private care seem so attractive. It is not at all unknown for doctors to invite patients to queue jump from their NHS list on to their private list in order to be seen quickly. Even though the private sector is so small – largely because of the perfectly adequate service that is offered to the public by the NHS – it allows the state service to act as its safety net and to cover the many gaps in the private service through which fee-paying patients might otherwise fall.

Private medicine can offer no cover, for example, for chronic conditions or for common circumstances such as maternity which might cripple it. To increase the private sector still further, as many people suggest, would make the health service even more divisive. The best service you can offer the poor – or the old or the chronic sick – is to include them in the same service as everyone else. The health services in Britain – or anywhere else – would not be improved by being turned into a two-tier system. Doctors themselves, in defence of a private sector, talk passionately about freedom in medicine, both for themselves and for the supposedly omniscient patient who is to choose freely among the best that medicine has to offer, but freedom is best preserved by removing professional decisions from immediate economic pressure. The individual contract between doctor and patient may offer an unparalleled opportunity for mutual trust and altruistic care, but it also offers an unparalleled opportunity for profiteering and quackery. Better the system which offers safeguards on medical practice and expenditure as well as attempting to safeguard the best of the doctor–patient relationship.

There is also a point of view which has no objection to the idea of a National Health Service that offers a universal service to everybody, with all the state control which that implies, but which feels, none the less, that its source of income ought somehow to be protected, ought to be lifted out of the political arena of Cabinet decisions and competition with other claims on the government's budget. When times are hard this point of view resents the fact that the health service faces cuts and squeezes along with less humanitarian and worthy sectors of the public service. This argument is in favour of a separate, protected health service fund, but it is based on two false premises. One is that the health service does suffer badly in times of financial stress when in fact it does comparatively well. 'There appears,' writes Rudolf Klein, 'to be a clash between the subjective sense of cataclysm among those working in the NHS and the objective evidence of the public expenditure figures.'[7] Professor Klein points out a rise of 23% *in real terms* in health service spending over the last five years and draws from it the conclusion that the NHS actually gets a high degree of priority in government spending, and even points out that at a time when our standard of living has actually dropped, the NHS is doing very well to be allocated a rising share of national income.

The other premise is that health services have a great effect on health. A National Health Service which considered itself above the struggle – or cooperation – with other interests in the community would be a National Health Service which was in danger of believing in medical mythology, a service which would base itself still further on the idea that curative medicine was what mattered, that the health of the community was a separate treatable entity, apart from education, housing, leisure, actual quality of life, even politics. It is not. Health is a correlate of all these things and it cannot be separated, either politically or financially. The National Union of Public Employees, in its evidence to the Royal Commission, states rather indigestibly but none the less with truth, that 'the total achievement of its (the health service's) object cannot be met by improvements in the National Health Service alone but will require accompanying improvements in the totality of those factors (for example levels of income and employment, housing, education, nutrition, working conditions, leisure facilities, etc.) which are directly related to the health of the community.' And in the sense in which the health of the community is inseparable from every other element of community life, health *is* politics.

The value of a country's health service cannot be judged entirely by mortality figures, by health statistics and spending levels. A health service deals with so many factors that are immeasurable, particularly in the caring rather than the curing side of its duties. And one must never forget the effect it has on the healthy population, the population which may not form part of the morbidity and mortality tables, statistics of days off, drugs taken and beds occupied. Professor Cochrane pointed out that there is more than one kind of output from the NHS, and it has an output that still isn't equalled by many other health services, whatever their statistics and cost-benefit analysis and their complement of scientific wonders.[8] This is the social output, the increased equality in a community that is based on universal access to health care, the freedom from stress and worry that results when that care is free of charge at point of access. The fact that the NHS is free at point of need, and available to anybody who needs it, is a social benefit of more importance than a particular new hospital or the facilities for treating a particular disease. Socially and morally, as well as financially, the NHS, for all its failings, is still a best buy. Despite its faults it does not yet sell its wares like potato chips to the highest bidder, and despite its inefficiencies, the system of payment through general taxation with control by democratic government still offers the most desirable balance of shared payment with public control. The system we have works imperfectly, and it is wracked with the symptoms of the health service disease, but it is not dead yet. It contains within its framework, within the minds of the people who work for it and the people who pay for and use it, the potential for recovery and growth guided by the light of the old ideal.

Certain measures, some of which have been touched on in this book, could help it on its way. The role of the medical profession is crucial. Without their cooperation the NHS could be wrecked. With it, it could still be the best health system in the world. The reform of medical education, starting with the selection of students who are not just academically bright but likely to be caring could be the basis of a new outlook in the medical profession. This could be consolidated by a much larger component of community medicine and health economics in the medical curriculum which would help to produce doctors with a sense of health service needs. And young doctors could be joined by a new style of health worker, those who already work in the service, particularly in deprived and backward areas, but who have been upgraded in a devolution of medical responsibility. The continued evaluation of medical procedures, with the aim of controlling medical inflation and improving the service, should be encouraged from within the profession, maybe with the establishment of a specific epidemiological unit within the Department of Health whose task was the organization and encouragement of scientific evaluation in the health service.

Financially, and administratively, there needs to be a much clearer line of authority from the centre out. Decisions in the health service shouldn't really be dependent on endless battles and lobbyings within infinite numbers of committees, despite the importance of the democratic voice. If and when the government makes decisions on priorities – if and when, for example, it decides to up-grade the geriatric service, to provide community care for the mentally ill – such decisions should be followed immediately and automatically by *protected* funds, by money that can't be nibbled away by voracious consultants from hungrier specialities. Unless this firm step is taken, any central decisions on policy are so much hot air. Likewise money should be specifically set aside for health education with increased emphasis on what we can positively do for ourselves. Time and money spent on improving morale within the service, on creating a sense of purpose among its disunited workers, by opening two-way channels for their ideas on improvement, would not be ill-spent. The continuation of private practice within the NHS can only act as a powerful brake on any improvement in morale among its workers, and on the equality of service given to its patients. The medical profession will need to be offered considerable financial incentives to abandon it but it may well be worth the price in the long term to produce a unified National Health Service that pulls forward with all possible power at the wheel. It's an old and creaking engine, but it's on the right tracks.

Notes

1 The Health Service Disease

1. Michael Foot, *Aneurin Bevan*, vol. 2, Davis Poynter, 1973.
2. Enoch Powell, *A New Look at Medicine and Politics*, Pitman Medical, 1966.
3. Robert Maxwell, *Health Care – the Growing Dilemma*, McKinsey, 1974.
4. H. Mahler, 'Health – a demystification of medical technology', *Lancet*, ii, 1975, 829.

2 A Purchasable Commodity

1. R. H .Tawney, *Equality*, Allen & Unwin, 1931.
2. *Priorities for Health and Personal Social Services*, HMSO, 1975.
3. *Public Expenditure on Health*, OECD, Paris, July 1977.
4. Enoch Powell, ibid.
5. David Owen, *In Sickness and in Health – the Politics of Medicine*, Quartet Books, 1976.
6. Julian Tudor Hart, 'The inverse care law', *Lancet*, i, 1971, 405.
7. National Federation of Women's Institutes, *Evidence to the Royal Commission on the National Health Service*, 1977.
8. D. Neuhauser and A. M. Lewicki, *New England Journal of Medicine*, 1975, 227, 293.
9. W. Card and G. H. Mooney, *British Medical Journal*, 2, 1977, 1627–9.

3 Doctor Power

1. Thomas McKeown, *The Role of Medicine: Dream, Mirage or Nemesis?* Nuffield Provincial Hospitals Trust, 1976.
2. *Report of the Royal Commission on Medical Education*, HMSO, 1968.
3. *Health, the People's Right* (Labour Party's evidence to the Royal Commission on the National Health Service), HMSO, 1977.

4 The Holes in the Net

1. D. Roe, *The Elderly: Social Trends*, HMSO, 1973.
2. Nicholas Bosanquet, *New Deal for the Elderly*, Fabian Tract 435, 1975.
3. ibid.
4. Barbara Robb, *Sans Everything: A case to answer*, Nelson, 1967.
5. Robert Maxwell, ibid.
6. Barbara Robb, ibid.

5 Stopping the Gaps

1. Robert Maxwell, ibid.
2. C. L. Rosenberg, *Medical Economics*, 13 September 1975.
3. Brian Abel Smith, *Value for Money in Health Services*, Heinemann, 1976.
4. K. A. M. Grant, 'Pilot project of MCH clinics in rural Ethiopia', MFCM unpublished dissertation, F.C.M., R.C.P., 1977.
5. Oscar Gish, *Doctor Migration and World Health* (Occasional Papers on Social Administration, 43), 1971.
6. Brian Abel Smith, ibid.
7. ibid.
8. ibid.
9. David Owen, ibid.
10. Z. Chowdhury, 'Tubectomies by paraprofessional surgeons in rural Bangladesh', *Lancet*, i, 1975, 567–70.
11. Brian Abel Smith, ibid.
12. W. O. Spitzer *et al.*, 'The Burlington randomized trial of the nurse-practitioner', *New England Journal of Medicine*, 1974, 251, 290.
13. D. L. Crombie, ed. Hauser, in *The Economics of Medical Care*, Allen & Unwin, 1972.
14. Alfred Sadler, Blair Sadler and Ann Bliss, *The Physician's Assistant: Today and Tomorrow*, Yale University Press, 1972.

6 Yes – But Does It Work?

1. Victor R. Fuchs, *Who Shall Live? Health Economics and Social Choice*, Basic Books, Inc., 1974.
2. *Newsweek*, 10 April 1978.

3. Berki, *Hospital Economics*, Lexington.

4. A. L. Cochrane, *Effectiveness and Efficiency: Random Reflections on Health Services*, Nuffield Provincial Hospitals Trust, 1971.

5. ibid.

6. H. G. Mather *et al.*, 'Acute myocardial infarction. Home and hospital treatment', *British Medical Journal*, 3, 1971, 334.

7. *Newsweek*, 10 April 1978.

8. A. L. Cochrane, ibid.

9. *Newsweek*, 10 April 1978.

10. M. S. Feldstein, *Economic Analysis for Health Service Efficiency*, North Holland, 1967.

11. J. L. Dawson *et al.*, 'Tuberculosis Chemotherapy Centre, Madras' (A five year study of patients with pulmonary tuberculosis – a current comparison of home and sanatorium treatment for one year with isoniazid plus P.A.S.), *Bulletin of the World Health Organization*, 34, 1966, 533.

12. Victor R. Fuchs, ibid.

13. Derek Dunlop, *Medicines in Our Time*, Nuffield Provincial Hospitals Trust, 1973.

14. *Guardian*, 3 February 1977.

15. D. M. Davies *et al.*, 'Comprehensive clinical drug information service: First year's experience,' *British Medical Journal*, 1, 1977, 89–90.

16. K. Dunnell and A. Cartwright, *Medicine Takers, Prescribers and Hoarders*, Routledge & Kegan Paul, 1972.

17. V. W. M. Drury, O. L. Wade and E. Woolf, 'Following advice in general practice', *Journal of the Royal College of General Practitioners*, 26, 1976, 712–18.

18. Elspeth T. Macdonald, J. B. Macdonald and Margaret Phoenix, 'Improving drug compliance after hospital discharge', *British Medical Journal*, 2, 618–21.

7 Democracy in the Health Service: The Professionals

1. J. Banham, *Evidence to the Royal Commission on the National Health Service*, 1977.

2. *New Bottles: Old Wine?* Institute for Health Studies, Hull, 1974.

3. ibid.

4. David Owen, ibid.

5. *British Medical Journal*, 2, 1977, 1637–42.

6. 'Making Welsh Health Authorities more democratic', Welsh Office, 1974.

8 Democracy in the Health Service: The Amateurs

1. M. E. J. Wadsworth, R. Blaney and W. J. H. Butterfield, *Health and Sickness: The Choice of Treatment*, Tavistock Publications, 1971.

2. K. Dunnell and A. Cartwright, ibid.

3. K. J. Roghmann and R. J. Haggerty, 'The diary as a research instrument in the study of health and illness behaviour', *Medical Care*, 1972, 142.

4. D. T. Jones, 'Consulting the public: some recent findings', *British Medical Journal*, 2, 1977, 1101.

5. J. Hallas, *CHCs in Action*, Nuffield Provincial Hospitals Trust, 1976.

9 Changing the Face of Medicine

1. R. Tawney, ibid.

2. Victor R. Fuchs, ibid.

3. Michael Grossman, *The Correlation Between Health and Schooling, Household Production and Consumption*, National Bureau of Economic Research.

4. Victor R. Fuchs, ibid.

5. *Prevention and Health: Everybody's Business*, HMSO, 1976.

6. Last, 'The clinical iceberg', *Lancet*, i, 1963.

7. W. W. Holland *et al.*, 'A controlled trial of multiphasic screening in middle age' (Results of the South East London screening study), *International Journal of Epidemiology*, December 1977.

8. J. Cutler *et al.*, 'Multiphasic check-up evaluation study', *Preventive Medicine*, 2, 1973, 197–246.

9. *World Health Organization Expert Committee on Drug Dependence*, 1974, 551.

10. Robert Maxwell, ibid.

11. Belloc, 'Relationship of health practice and mortality', *Preventive Medicine*, 2, 1973, 67–81.

10   Paying the Piper

1. *Newsweek*, 10 April 1978.

2. Herbert Klarman, 'The difference the third party makes', *Journal of Risk and Insurance*, no. 5. December 1969, 36.

3. Bernard Friedman, 'A test of alternative demand-shift response to the Medicare Program', unpublished paper delivered at the International Economic Association Conference, Tokyo, 1973.

4. *Newsweek*, 10 April 1978.

5. Robert Maxwell, ibid.

6. Rudolf Klein, 'International perspectives on the NHS', *British Medical Journal*, 3.12.1977.

7. Rudolf Klein, 'NHS expenditure: turning figures into facts', *British Medical Journal*, 26.3.1977.

8. A. L. Cochrane, ibid.

Index

More About Penguins
and Pelicans

Penguinews, which appears every month, contains details of all the new books issued by Penguins as they are published. It is supplemented by our stocklist, which includes almost 5,000 titles.

A specimen copy of *Penguinews* will be sent to you free on request. Please write to Dept EP, Penguin Books Ltd, Harmondsworth, Middlesex, for your copy.

In the U.S.A.: For a complete list of books available from Penguins in the United States write to Dept CS, Penguin Books, 625 Madison Avenue, New York, New York 10022.

In Canada: For a complete list of books available from Penguins in Canada write to Penguin Books Canada Ltd, 2801 John Street, Markham, Ontario L3R 1B4.

In Australia: For a complete list of books published by Penguins in Australia write to the Marketing Department, Penguin Books Australia Ltd, P.O. Box 257, Ringwood, Victoria 3134.

Health Rights Handbook
A Guide to Medical Care
Gerry and Carol Stimson

A completely up-to-date guide to the medical facilities available to you in Britain. The authors believe that *your body belongs to you and only you should decide what to do with it and what to have done with it*. Their book will help you to understand the NHS itself and to deal with doctors and other health workers in order to get the most out the services available.

Our Bodies Ourselves
A Health Book by and for women
Boston Women's Health Book Collective
British Edition by Angela Phillips and Jill Rakusen

The most successful book about women ever published, *Our Bodies Ourselves* has sold over one million copies worldwide.
'Every woman in the country should be issued with a copy free of charge' – *Mother and Baby*
'Well researched, informative and educational for both men and women' – *British Medical Journal*
'The Bible of the woman's health movement' – *Guardian*
'If there's only one book you ever buy – this should be it' – *19*

and two Penguin Reference books

The Penguin Medical Encyclopedia
Peter Wingate (Second Edition 1976)

This encyclopedia which has been revised and updated is addressed to anyone who is concerned with the care of sick people and in particular to the patient himself, without being a 'do-it-yourself' medical manual. Hundreds of entries deal with the body and mind in health and sickness. With drugs and surgery, with the history institutions and vocabulary of the profession and with many other aspects of medical science.

Medicines: A Guide for Everybody
Peter Parish (Second edition 1979)

A unique guide to virtually every commonly used medicine and drug in Britain today. It is designed to tell the ordinary reader in ordinary language when it is desirable or useful to take a drug or to consult a doctor about a prescription; what specific drugs really do: how to ensure appropriate dosage; how to minimize side-effects; how to liaise with a doctor or pharmacist.

Penguins for Parents

From the author of The Experience of Childbirth

The Experience of Breastfeeding

Sheila Kitzinger

This comprehensive, up-to-date and thoroughly practical book includes all the recent research on the newborn baby's abilities and on the vital parent-child relationship, and explores sympathetically the stresses involved for both parents. Mrs Kitzinger looks too at the mass of new evidence on the advantages of breastfeeding, at the constituents of breast milk and the effects of drugs upon it, and discusses the dangers of artificial feeding in Third World countries.

Baby & Child

Penelope Leach

'A first-rate handbook of childcare and is, in my view, to be wholly recommended to anyone expecting a baby or who has one already. It stands head and shoulders above anything else of the same type that is available at the moment. It is clear, easy to understand, well-written and excellently informed ... I know I will look it up again and again' – Mary Kenny in the *Spectator*

Babyhood

Infant Development from Birth to Two Years

Penelope Leach

Why do babies cry? What is a 'good mixed diet' and is it necessary? Are boys and girls different in mind as well as body? In this account of the developments which turn a helpless newborn babe into a roving, chattering, almost-human two-year-old, Dr Leach distils the mountain of recent research to give the *facts* – the hows and whys of infant development as far as they are understood; the pros and cons of different kinds of child-rearing as far as they have been studied.

'Contains much useful information in a highly readable form ... Highly recommended' – *Mother and Baby*

Toddlers and Parents
T. Berry Brazelton

Bewildered, anxious, amused, exhausted by your toddler? Each chapter in this indispensable guide focusses on a special problem: working parents, single parents, large families, disturbed families, hyperactive children, toddler rivalry, and the use of day nurseries, playgroups and minders. Interspersed with the descriptions are reassuring, practical analyses of the toddler's psychological motivation and sympathetic, constructive comments on the parents' reactions.

Nurseries Now
A Fair Deal for Parents and Children
Hughes, Mayall, Perry, Petrie and Pinkerton

The need for nurseries is greater in Britain now than ever before. *Nurseries Now* combines a consumer's guide to what nurseries are available with a sensible critique of the gaps and anomalies in the present system. The authors emphasize the importance of equal opportunities, of more choice for parents in child-care, and of a greater involvement by men in their children's upbringing. Nurseries alone cannot achieve these aims, and the book also looks at some of the other measures needed, including radical changes in the employment patterns of both sexes.

Children in their Primary Schools
Henry Pluckrose

In this introduction to the many methods which abound in English primary schools, Henry Pluckrose discusses both the content of the curriculum and the philosophy which underlies it. He points out the relative merits of rigid and freer time-tables, and shows us how play and work are equally essential, can be equally educative, and in many cases are actually interchangeable. He also explores the current problems and looks ahead to the changes we can expect in the next ten years.

Clever Children in Comprehensive Schools
Auriol Stevens

Do you wilfully sacrifice bright children for political principles if you send them to a comprehensive school? In this sane and well-balanced assessment of comprehensive and selective school methods, the education correspondent of the *Observer* gives the facts – about mixed ability teaching, about the minimum size for a comprehensive with a good sixth form, about the challenge of research versus the slog of disciplined work, about provision for science and language teaching. She is sensitive both to the dilemma that faces parents as well as to the problems met by teachers who strive to fulfil the varied needs of their pupils.

Progress for a Small Planet
Barbara Ward

In the seven years that Barbara Ward and René Dubos's *Only One Earth* has been a bestseller, we have become more familiar with environmental problems and global tensions. Three dominate the headlines: pollution, the energy crisis and the poverty of our developing nations. Some claim such crises are insoluble, others that new technologies hold the answers.

In this masterly survey of possible policies, Barbara Ward outlines the planetary bargain between the world's nations that would guarantee every citizen the right to freedom from poverty and keep our shared biosphere in good, working order.

Britain in Agony
The Growth of Political Violence
Richard Clutterbuck

During the 1970s violent picketing, demonstrations and terrorism reached their highest peak in Britain since 1911. Richard Clutterbuck looks at the events, from the IRA bombings in Birmingham to the Grunwick dispute and the NP/SWP confrontations in Lewisham and Ladywood, and analyses their underlying causes in the context of recent developments in the political economy – the Industrial Relations Act, the Social Contract and runaway inflation. The lesson he draws stands out stark and clear.

Just and Unjust Wars
A Moral Argument with Historical Illustrations
Michael Walzer

Can a war ever be just? And if so, does that justify unjust actions which may – or may not – bring it to a speedier end? Drawing on historical illustrations ranging from the Athenian attack on Melos to the My Lai massacre, Michael Walzer analyzes the moral judgements that people have actually made in battle and at time of war to reaffirm the argument for justice against the 'realists' who claim that winning is all.

'A magnificent book, an honour to its writer . . . that makes for a return of civilized discussion of the question of the morality of warfare' – *New York Review of Books*